Provided
by

Measure B

which was approved by
the voters in
November, 1998

Brown v. Board of Education:
separate but equal?

SUPREME COURT MILESTONES

Brown v. Board of Education:

separate but equal?

SUSAN DUDLEY GOLD

BENCHMARK BOOKS

MARSHALL CAVENDISH
NEW YORK

For my nephew, Damon R. Gray

*With special thanks to Professor David M. O'Brien of the
Woodrow Wilson Department of Politics at the University of
Virginia for reviewing the text of this book*

Benchmark Books · Marshall Cavendish · 99 White Plains Road · Tarrytown, NY 10591
www.marshallcavendish.com · Copyright © 2005 by Susan Dudley Gold · All rights
reserved. No part of this book may be reproduced or utilized in any form or by any
means electronic or mechanical including photocopying, recording, or by any information
storage and retrieval system, without permission from the copyright holders. · Library
of Congress Cataloging-in-Publication Data · Gold, Susan Dudley. · Brown v. Board of
Education : separate but equal? / by Susan Dudley Gold. · p. cm. — (Supreme Court
milestones) · Includes bibliographical references and index. · ISBN 0-7614-1842-3
1. Brown, Oliver, 1918—-Trials, litigation, etc.—Juvenile literature. 2. Topeka (Kan.).
Board of Education—Trials, litigation, etc.—Juvenile literature. 3. Segregation in education—
Law and legislation—United States—Juvenile literature. 4. African Americans—Civil
rights—Juvenile literature. I. Title: Brown versus Board of Education. II. Title. III. Series.
KF228.B76G65 2005\ · 344.73'0798—dc22 · 2004005866

All Internet sites were available and accurate when sent to press.

Photo Research by Candlepants Incorporated

Cover photo: Thurgood Marshall (center) flanked by George E. C. Hayes (left) and James
Nabrit Jr., the lawyers who argued *Brown* v. *Board of Education*.

Cover Photo: Corbis/Bettmann

The photographs in this book are used by permission and through the courtesy of:
Corbis: Bettmann, 2/3, 29 80, 85, 89, 96, 99, 110, 112, 117; *Carl Iwasaki/Time Life
Pictures/Getty Images*: 6, 10; *Photographs and Prints Division, Schomburg Center for
Research in Black Culture, The New York Public Library, Astor, Lenox and Tilden
Foundations*: 18; *Library of Congress*: (LC-USF34-046248) 21, (LC-USZ62-84479) 38,
(LC-USZ62-126449) 41, (LC-USZ62-112522) 51, (LC-USZ62-113498) 59; *Collection of
the Supreme Court of the United States*: 66, 70.

Series design by Sonia Chaghatzbanian
Printed in China
1 3 5 6 4 2

contents

LINDA BROWN (LEFT) AND HER SIX-YEAR-OLD SISTER, TERRY LYNN, WALK ALONG
THE RAILROAD TRACKS TO THE BUS THAT WILL TAKE THEM TO A SEGREGATED SCHOOL
FAR FROM THE "WHITES ONLY" SCHOOL IN THEIR NEIGHBORHOOD.

one
A Girl and a Dream

seven-year-old Linda Brown had to walk six blocks through a dangerous railroad yard to catch a bus. Then she had to ride for about a mile to get to Monroe School, where she attended third grade. Her journey began at 7:40 a.m. She finally entered her classroom at 9 a.m.

Another school, Sumner Elementary School, was much closer—less than four blocks from her home in Topeka, Kansas. But school officials would not allow Linda to attend the school in her neighborhood. That was because she was black, and Sumner School was for white students only. In 1950, the year Linda's story begins, junior and senior high schools in Kansas accepted both black and white students. Elementary schools, however, were segregated.

Linda's father, the Reverend Oliver Brown, decided to take action. One morning in early September 1950, he and Linda walked to Sumner School. When they got there, Linda waited outside while her father went to ask the principal if his little girl could attend Sumner, which was nearby, instead of Monroe, which was much farther away. The principal quickly denied the request. An angry Brown left the room and walked home with Linda.

For more than two centuries, a huge divide had separated blacks from whites in America. First brought to the country as slaves, blacks had labored in cotton fields and inside plantations, serving white masters. The Civil War freed them from slavery but offered little to help them improve their lot. In most of the South, blacks could not stay in hotels open to whites. They were barred from restaurants, restrooms, and swimming pools where whites gathered. They had to use separate drinking fountains and ride in the back of public buses.

In seventeen states, laws required black and white students to attend separate schools. Four other states and the District of Columbia allowed local school boards to separate students by race.

Many people in the North and the South objected to the way blacks were treated and to the laws that allowed such treatment. They believed that segregation—separating people by race—violated the Constitution. Written by America's leading thinkers in 1787, the U.S. Constitution has been in force longer than any other written constitution in the world. It lays out the basic principles of law on which the United States was founded.

Those who supported segregation argued that separation by race was fair to both blacks and whites. They pointed to an 1896 Supreme Court ruling in *Plessy* v. *Ferguson* that upheld the doctrine of "separate but equal." Under the doctrine, blacks could be separated from whites as long as they had equal facilities and schools. Although sometimes this was true, in the vast majority of cases, the schools and services reserved for blacks were far from equal to those provided for whites.

At the time, few Southern blacks were allowed to vote. White leaders seldom responded to complaints from blacks. Those few who did found that white citizens cast their votes for someone else on election day. Black leaders and their supporters would eventually look to the nation's courts in the long battle to end segregation.

THE NAACP SEEKS JUSTICE

The National Association for the Advancement of Colored People (NAACP), founded by a multiracial group of men and women in 1909, led the push to desegregate public schools in the United States. From its first year in operation, the NAACP had sought justice for black Americans in the courts. In addition, the organization worked for voting rights for black Americans and for equal treatment in the criminal justice system and employment. Much of its work in the 1920s and 1930s focused on antilynching laws. In 1940, the NAACP formed the Legal Defense and Educational Fund, Inc., to handle litigation for the organization. It was this branch of the NAACP that handled the school discrimination cases.

Under the U.S. justice system, a court will hear a civil case only if a person who is directly involved files suit. To get into court, the NAACP in Kansas had to find parents and students willing to lend their names to the case against school segregation. Oliver Brown, Linda's father, agreed to join the NAACP's battle. He would allow the organization to pursue the case on his and Linda's behalf.

Twelve mothers in other parts of the city had also asked that their children be allowed to attend local schools. They received the same answer as the Browns. The doors of Topeka's white elementary schools were closed to black children. The thirteen black parents, backed by the NAACP's legal defense branch, appealed to the Topeka School Board. The board rejected their plea. State law, the board noted, gave the board the power to separate elementary students by race.

The parents took their appeal to federal court. On February 28, 1951, NAACP lawyers filed suit in the U.S. District Court for Kansas. Brown agreed to head the list

LINDA BROWN (THIRD FROM LEFT) AND OTHER CHILDREN WHO WERE PART OF THE *BROWN* CHALLENGE TO SEGREGATED SCHOOLS.

of plaintiffs in the case, and it became known as *Brown* v. *Board of Education of Topeka*. Other black men and women who had taken stands for equality had lost their jobs and been harassed. Brown, however, seemed less likely to become a target than most. As a minister in the African Methodist Episcopal (AME) Church in Topeka, he had the respect of the community. He had served in the armed forces, held a union job as a welder, and had never belonged to the NAACP. He was not seen as a troublemaker.

For Linda

Brown later said he took on the battle for his daughter. "She seems very apt," he said. "I want her to have something more to look forward to than washing dishes."

Not everyone in the black community applauded the action. Many feared local whites would harass them because of the suit. Some people believed their children would be better off attending all-black schools. They did not want their children to face abuse from angry white students. Others believed the suit cast doubt on the skills of the excellent black teachers who taught at the city's all-black schools.

Those joining Brown in the suit included Lucinda Todd, secretary of the Topeka NAACP, whose daughter also had been denied access to a nearby white school. But most of the others in the suit, like Brown, had no ties to the NAACP. All their children had to travel far beyond white schools in their own neighborhoods to attend all-black schools.

As the NAACP lawyers guided the *Brown* case through the legal system, similar suits were being filed in other states. Eventually, five of these cases would be combined and argued as one before the Supreme Court under the name *Brown* v. *Board of Education*.

JOINING THE FRAY

By 1951, campaigns to desegregate the schools had sprung up in several states. Two battles focused on Delaware: one in Claymont, a suburb of Wilmington, and one in the rural town of Hockessin. The first state to ratify the U.S. Constitution, Delaware lay between the North and the South. During the Civil War the state remained with the Union, although it allowed slavery. Following the war, Delaware—like Southern states— kept blacks and whites apart in restaurants, theaters, hospitals, and practically every other public building. And like the laws in many Southern states, Delaware's Constitution required separate schools for both blacks and whites.

MORE CLASSES AND A RIDE TO SCHOOL

In 1951, Ethel Belton and seven other black parents in Claymont wanted their children to go to a better school. Howard High, where the town's black students attended classes, was overcrowded and offered only a limited number of courses. The school was in a poor section of Wilmington, far from most students' homes. In con- trast, white students went to a new school in Claymont. There they studied Spanish, economics, and other advanced classes. After school, the students could choose from activities ranging from driver's education to working on the school newspaper.

That same year, Sarah Bulah had a different prob- lem with her daughter's school. Her family lived in the small rural community of Hockessin. Every morning

Bulah had to drive her ten-year-old daughter Shirley two miles to the old one-room schoolhouse reserved for blacks because the school had no bus. A school bus passed the Bulah home every day, carrying white students to their school.

Tired of driving her daughter to school, Bulah asked school officials to let Shirley ride on the white students' bus. If white students had a bus take them to school, she reasoned, then black students should also be able to ride a bus. When the local authorities turned down her request, she took her case to state officials and the governor. They told Bulah that "colored" (as African Americans were referred to at that time) students weren't allowed to ride on a bus reserved for whites. They made no move to provide a separate bus for black students.

Both the Claymont parents and Sarah Bulah asked a Wilmington lawyer, Louis Redding, for legal advice. Redding, the first black lawyer to practice in Delaware, had won a case the year before for black college students. As a result of the case, the state court had ordered the University of Delaware to accept black students for the first time.

At Redding's advice, the parents filed formal requests with the state board of education to admit their children to the local white schools. It was no surprise when the board turned down the requests. Redding appealed to the state's appeals court, called the Chancery Court, asking that the ruling be overturned. The suit named the state board of education as the defendant. Board member Francis B. Gebhart appeared first on the list, so the suits became known as *Belton* v. *Gebhart* and *Bulah* v. *Gebhart*.

students strike

Black students in Farmville, Virginia, waged their own battle against substandard schools. In the spring of 1950, Barbara Rose Johns, a black high school student, led 116 other students in a strike protesting the poor condition of their school. The school, Moton High School, was located in Prince Edward County. Rundown and overcrowded, the school had originally been partly funded by a black women's club. The building lacked space for all the county's black students. Students were forced to attend classes in tar-paper shacks that had no toilets. Woodstoves provided the only heat during cold winters. The white high school offered many courses that Moton did not—physics, world history, Latin, advanced typing and stenography, drawing, woodworking, metalworking, and machine shop work.

At the time, Virginia provided schools for blacks only through the eighth grade. County school boards oversaw the schools. High schools run by churches and private organizations enabled black students to extend their education. The principal of Moton High and the president of the local NAACP, who also headed the school's parent-teacher organization, asked the county board to upgrade the school to equal the white students' school.

The school board took no action in the matter. Frustrated, the students went on strike for two weeks. They returned to school only after the NAACP promised to argue their case. That May, lawyer Spottswood Robinson filed suit in federal court on the students' behalf. Because ninth-grade student Dorothy Davis's name appeared first on the list of students, the case became known as *Dorothy E. Davis* v. *County School Board of Prince Edward County*.

A Broken-Down Bus and Wood Shacks

Black children in Clarendon County, South Carolina, went to school in wood shacks. The impoverished black schools, many set up by black churches, had little money to pay teachers and buy supplies and textbooks. Children had to walk as much as eight miles to school because there were no buses.

The Reverend J. A. DeLaine, who taught at St. Paul Rural Primary School in Clarendon County, asked county school officials to provide a bus for the students at the school. When the officials refused, DeLaine and other blacks wrote to state officials, but they, too, denied the request. In desperation, black parents bought a used school bus for the school. When the bus broke down, the parents could not afford to have it repaired.

The local school officials had told DeLaine that black children weren't entitled to a bus because their parents didn't contribute enough in taxes to cover the cost. White parents, the officials said, shouldn't be expected to pay for a bus for black children.

DeLaine won support for his case from the national NAACP, whose lawyers filed the case, *Briggs* v. *Elliott*, in U.S. District Court in 1950. Thurgood Marshall, lead counsel for the NAACP Legal Defense Fund, and South Carolina attorney Harold Boulware represented the plaintiffs. The suit was named for Harry Briggs, one of the parents who joined DeLaine and eighteen others in the suit. R. W. Elliot, named as the defendant in the case, served as president of Clarendon County's school board.

The plaintiffs asked the court to provide black children in the county with schools equal to those of whites. School officials claimed the district already provided equal facilities. Marshall decided to challenge the state's segregation laws themselves, asking that public schools be open to all. Since the suit involved a state statute that conflicted with constitutional rights, the case was moved to a three-judge panel.

A Lawyer For $14

Like many other parts of the country, Washington, D.C., placed little importance on the education of black youths. In 1950 black students in the nation's capital crammed into rundown schools that offered few courses and none of the after-school programs available at white schools in the city. Schools for blacks often ran double and triple sessions to make room for all the students.

Gardner Bishop, a local barber and father, spearheaded a protest among poor black parents who wanted better schools for their children. In 1948, he organized a monthlong student strike at Browne Junior High School to protest poor conditions at the black school. When that produced no results, Bishop visited renowned civil rights lawyer Charles Houston to ask for help. Impressed by Bishop's determination, Houston asked him how much money his group had to spend. "Fourteen dollars," Bishop replied. "Well," said Houston, "you've got yourself a lawyer."

Houston arranged for Bishop to call off the student strike. In return, the lawyer pledged to file suit in an effort to win equal education for blacks in the city. In taking the case to court, Houston faced many hurdles. For one, Congress had for years approved segregated schools for the city. For another, the Fourteenth Amendment, which said that states could not deprive citizens of their rights, did not apply to Washington, D.C., which was under Congress's jurisdiction.

When Houston became too ill to continue with the case, James M. Nabrit Jr. took over. Nabrit, a brilliant professor who would soon become president of Howard University, expanded the case. He believed the fight had to center on ending segregation and foresaw that the battle would ultimately be fought in the Supreme Court.

On September 11, 1950, Bishop led eleven black students to John Philip Sousa Junior High School, a large new school built for white students in the area. When Bishop's group asked that the students be allowed to attend, school officials turned them down. They took their campaign to the board of education, whose president, C. Melvin Sharpe, also rejected their request. That set the stage for Nabrit's suit in U.S. District Court, which he filed as *Bolling* v. *Sharpe* in early 1951. Twelve-year-old Spottswood Thomas Bolling Jr. had been among those accompanying Bishop to Sousa Junior High School.

As these cases slowly made their way through the court system, black students continued to struggle with the inequities of segregation and poor schools. By 1952, the state cases would be joined as *Brown* v. *Board of Education*. The Supreme Court's decision in the consolidated case would shake up American education as never before. The *Bolling* case, too, would make its mark at the Supreme Court.

ELECTIONEERING AT THE SOUTH.—Sketched by W. L. Sheppard.—[See Page 467.]

After the Civil War, African Americans were given the vote in the South and were wooed by "electioneers," as shown in this wood engraving from *Harper's Weekly* magazine, July 25, 1868.

TWO
CIVIL WAR LEGACY

THE SCHOOL DESEGREGATION CASES of the 1950s and the injustices they revealed were rooted in the social upheaval of the previous century. The victory of the North in the Civil War freed the slaves and left white Southerners bitter and determined to regain power.

After the war, the federal government took control of the South. This period, known as Reconstruction, lasted from 1865 to 1877. Two factions in Congress vied for control during this period. The Radical Republicans wanted to make certain that the wealthy plantation owners of the old South did not win back control. They supported equal rights for black citizens and pushed for adoption of the Thirteenth Amendment, which abolished slavery. The Moderates' main goal was to restore the political rights of the Southern states. They cared far less about the plight of blacks in the South.

In 1865, the former Confederate states abolished slavery and, with the exception of Mississippi, ratified the Thirteenth Amendment. In exchange, President Andrew Johnson allowed the states to run their own affairs once again. White plantation owners, later pardoned by President Johnson, won election to local offices. The new state legislatures quickly enacted laws to keep black citizens from gaining power. Under these laws, called the black codes, blacks could not own land, vote, carry arms, or move about freely. Although these laws were later revoked, they served as a model for "Jim Crow" laws that discriminated against blacks and segregated them from whites. Many of these laws remained on the books until the mid-1960s. The term Jim Crow—a racial slur—originally came from a black character in minstrel shows performed during the 1830s.

BLACKS WIN RIGHTS

The Radical Republicans in Congress refused to seat the newly elected Southern members. In 1866, Congress passed a Civil Rights Act that granted citizenship to blacks and protected them from the black codes in force in the South. To further ensure that blacks received equal treatment, the Radical Republicans pushed passage of the Fourteenth Amendment. Under the amendment, "all persons born or naturalized in the United States"—including blacks—were automatically citizens who were guaranteed equal protection under the law. States could not deprive citizens of their rights, and Congress had the power to enforce the amendment's provisions. All of the former Confederate states except Tennessee refused to ratify the amendment.

Angered by this act of defiance, the Radical Republicans passed the Reconstruction Act in 1867, followed shortly by three related acts. The acts placed the Southern states, with the exception of Tennessee, under military control. In order to be accepted into the Union as independent states, the Southern states had to ratify the Fourteenth Amendment and adopt new constitutions.

President Johnson opposed the Radical Republicans' harsh treatment of the South. This disagreement eventually led to his impeachment in February 1868. He escaped con-

ONCE WHITES REGAINED POWER IN THE SOUTH, JIM CROW LAWS FLOURISHED. SEGREGATION IN THE SCHOOLS TOOK EFFECT, WITH BLACK CHILDREN COMMONLY TAUGHT IN LARGE NUMBERS BY ONE TEACHER IN CROWDED SCHOOLROOMS SUCH AS THIS ONE IN VEAZY, NORTH CAROLINA, 1941.

viction by one vote, but the controversy left him powerless to oppose Reconstruction further. In July 1868, the Fourteenth Amendment was ratified. Black voters helped elect the Radical Republican-backed candidate for president in 1868, Ulysses S. Grant.

By 1870 all the Southern states had been readmitted to the Union. That same year, the Fifteenth Amendment, guaranteeing black males the right to vote, became the law of the land. Boosted by black votes, Radical Republicans gained control of the government in the South.

During this time, the Radical Republicans set up a Freedman's Bureau to provide food, shelter, jobs, and education for blacks and poor whites in the South. Before the Civil War, laws in a number of Southern states made it illegal to educate black children. Few knew how to read or write. By the 1880s, about a third of black children attended school in the South. For the first time, blacks took an active role in the public life of the South. They opened businesses, served on juries, and voted. Black officials filled posts in local government. Voters elected two black men to the U.S. Senate and seventeen to the House of Representatives.

WHITES REGAIN POWER

Many of the white men who had controlled the South before the Civil War resented the new role of black citizens. Their bitterness found a voice in the Ku Klux Klan and other groups willing to use violence to regain control. They terrorized blacks and their supporters throughout the South and in some Northern areas as well. The violence and threats kept fearful black citizens from jobs, voting booths, and other public activities.

Politics also played a role in weakening civil rights for blacks. Corruption and mismanagement in the Grant administration turned voters against Republicans. In the presidential election of 1876, a slim majority (51 percent) of Americans cast their votes for Samuel J. Tilden, the Democratic candidate. Returns in three states, however, were contested. Congress appointed a fifteen-member electoral commission to name the winner. The commission chose the Republican candidate, Rutherford B. Hayes. The vote was cast along party lines, with the eight Republicans voting in favor of Hayes and the seven Democrats supporting Tilden. After a lengthy debate, the Senate confirmed the commission's vote, and Hayes became president. According to some historians, Hayes made a deal with Southerners to withdraw federal troops from the South in exchange for their support. Other experts point out that Hayes had already pledged during the campaign to withdraw the last of the troops from the South. With either scenario, the result was the same: U.S. troops left the South.

Without protection from the federal government, blacks soon became the targets of powerful whites determined to win back control. White officials redrew voting district lines to favor white candidates. This practice, called gerrymandering, ensured that whites would win a majority of the seats in local and state elections.

Other tactics prevented blacks from voting at all. Polling places were located far from black neighborhoods. New laws required blacks to pay costly poll taxes before they could vote. Black voters were also forced to take literacy tests graded by white election officials. In Louisiana, for example, white lawmakers passed a "grandfather clause" that allowed illiterate citizens to vote if their fathers or grandfathers had been registered voters before 1867. Since blacks did not have the right to vote before 1867, the clause barred all illiterate blacks from the polls. Before the clause went into effect, 130,000 black citizens were registered to vote in Louisiana. After the clause, only 5,300 blacks remained on the state's voter registration list.

setbacks in court

Southern blacks did not fare much better in the courts. A series of Supreme Court decisions beginning in 1873 seriously weakened the position of blacks.

In March 1869 the Louisiana legislature granted exclusive rights to the Crescent City Live-Stock Landing and Slaughter-House Company to run slaughterhouses in a section of the state that included the city of New Orleans. Other slaughterhouse companies objected and filed suit. The U.S. Supreme Court heard the arguments in the suits—which became known as the *Slaughterhouse* cases—in 1872 and 1873. The plaintiffs argued that the Fourteenth Amendment prevented states from interfering with their right to make a living. They also claimed the Louisiana law denied them "equal protection of the laws" and deprived them of liberty and property "without due process of law," in violation of the Fourteenth Amendment.

The plaintiffs lost the case. In its April 14, 1873, decision, the Court ruled that the Fourteenth Amendment was written to protect only former slaves and applied only to *national* rights. So, for example, the amendment guaranteed black citizens the right to vote in national elections or equal treatment in making contracts with the federal government. But, according to the ruling, the amendment did not apply to state contracts, state elections, or other matters overseen by the state—or the states' control over the civil rights of their citizens.

In his dissent, Justice Stephen Field noted that Section 1 of the Fourteenth Amendment barred states from passing laws that interfered with the "privileges or immunities" of U.S. citizens. Field argued that the clause protected the privileges and immunities of all Americans— not just former slaves and not only national rights. The right of employment fell into that category, he said. Future rulings would add a long list of civil rights from housing to equal education and many other basics of life. However, Field was in the minority, and the limits imposed by the 1873 ruling would remain in effect for decades.

The decision had disastrous effects on the newly won rights of blacks. The 1873 Supreme Court's interpretation of the Fourteenth Amendment allowed states to pass a host of laws that discriminated against blacks on the local and state level. For example, states had full authority to operate separate schools for blacks. They could set their own voting regulations for state and local elections, designed to discourage blacks from voting. And they could enforce many state regulations in ways that barred blacks and others from good jobs and equal pay.

In a follow-up case in 1875, the Supreme Court ruled that states had control over state and local elections. The decision in the case, *U.S.* v. *Reese*, upheld the right of Kentucky to prevent a black man from voting in a local election.

In 1883 the Court ruled that the Civil Rights Act of 1875 was unconstitutional. The act had guaranteed the right of all people, regardless of race or color, "full and equal enjoyment" of public buildings, inns, theaters, hired cabs, and the like. In knocking down the act, the Court once again put severe limits on the reach of the Fourteenth Amendment. According to the Court, the amendment did not apply to "social rights," such as equal access to facilities. The decision further eroded black rights by allowing private businesses and people to discriminate against blacks.

A KILLIΠG BLOW

The Court's decision in *Plessy* v. *Ferguson* in 1896 delivered a killing blow to civil rights for blacks. The ruling set the standard for legal actions on the issue for almost six decades. The case related to an 1890 Louisiana law that required blacks and whites to ride in "equal but separate" railroad cars. In June 1892, Homer Adolph Plessy bought a first-class ticket and boarded the East Louisiana Railway coach reserved for whites. According to Court records, Plessy was "seven-eighths Caucasian and one-eighth African blood." Under state law, he was considered black. The conductor ordered Plessy to move to the section for black passengers. When he refused, a railway detective arrested him. Judge John H. Ferguson of

Louisiana's criminal district court found Plessy guilty.

Plessy's appeal found its way to the Supreme Court, where the justices ruled against him. In making their case, Plessy's lawyers argued that Louisiana's law violated both the Thirteenth and the Fourteenth Amendments.

The Court's majority decision quickly dispensed with the Thirteenth Amendment argument, noting that the amendment related to slavery and did not apply to the case.

The Fourteenth Amendment, according to the ruling, did not require states' laws to be color-blind. In particular, separate schools for black and white children had long been permitted. Justice Henry Billings Brown, in writing the decision, cited an 1850 Boston case, *Roberts* v. *City of Boston*. In that case, the Massachusetts supreme judicial court ruled that the Boston school committee held the power to segregate schools. Likewise, the U.S. Congress had required separate schools for blacks and whites in Washington, D.C. Other courts, Brown noted, had upheld state laws forbidding marriage between blacks and whites.

In the *Plessy* case, the Supreme Court once again limited the scope of the Fourteenth Amendment to national rights. Because the East Louisiana Railway operated only within the state of Louisiana, the rights guaranteed by the Fourteenth Amendment did not apply. The ruling went beyond previous decisions by allowing discrimination by public as well as private entities.

In issuing the decision, Justice Brown wrote the words that would lock segregation in place for the next half a century.

[W]e think the enforced separation of the races, as applied to the internal commerce of the state, neither abridges the privileges or immunities of the colored man, deprives him of his property without due process of law, nor denies him the equal protection of the laws, within the meaning of the fourteenth amendment.

Near the end of the ruling, Brown noted that if whites thought blacks were inferior to them, the Constitution could not eliminate the social prejudices of whites toward blacks. Acceptance of blacks as equals, he wrote, would have to take place voluntarily. "If one race be inferior to the other socially, the Constitution of the United States cannot put them upon the same plane."

A STINGING DISSENT

Justice John Marshall Harlan issued a stinging dissent to the decision. A dissent opposes the majority decision and includes reasons to bolster that view. The purpose behind the law, Harlan noted, was to force black riders "to keep to themselves" while aboard the train—thus limiting their freedom of movement. The Louisiana law and others like it, he said, were "inconsistent not only with that equality of rights which pertains to citizenship, national and state, but with the personal liberty enjoyed by everyone within the United States."

Almost sixty years later, civil rights lawyers arguing for school desegregation would echo Harlan's stand against segregation. "Our constitution is color-blind, and neither knows nor tolerates classes among citizens," wrote Harlan. "In respect of civil rights, all citizens are equal before the law. The humblest is the peer of the most powerful. The law regards man as man, and takes no account of his surroundings or of his color when his civil rights as guaranteed by the supreme law of the land are involved." He noted, "The arbitrary separation of citizens on the basis of race cannot be justified upon any legal grounds."

segregation laws

Many black farm workers in the South lost their jobs after the boll weevil seriously damaged cotton crops in 1915. Over the next several years, more than 400,000 workers went north to find jobs in the factories there. This movement was so large that it became known as the Great Migration. Like other newcomers, the black workers clustered together with those of the same ethnic background in poor areas of the cities. Although most Northern states did not have laws requiring segregation, in many areas blacks and whites were in fact separated. In many cases, homeowners in white neighborhoods would not sell housing to black families. Because children attended neighborhood schools, black children went to schools near their homes that were almost all black, while white children attended schools in their area that were almost exclusively white.

Some blacks moved to Southern cities to work in the factories that had spread there beginning in the early 1900s. The competition for jobs pitted black and white workers against each other in both the North and the South. White supremacist groups like the Ku Klux Klan, which experienced a rebirth in the 1920s, fanned the flames of suspicion and fear. These groups warned that blacks would eventually take over by marrying whites and having babies of mixed race.

White leaders responded to these fears by passing more laws separating the races. The federal government ordered the Post Office, the Department of the Treasury, and the Bureau of the Census to segregate. Black workers were forced to work behind curtains and were not allowed in company cafeterias. Banks, insurance companies, and labor unions discriminated against black clients and workers. Lynchings and terrorist acts against blacks increased.

jim crow reigns

Jim Crow laws flourished in the South. Proponents used a mix of arguments to justify such laws. Among them:

- Segregation prevented "race-mixing" (interracial marriages) and preserved the identity of each race.

- Without segregation, there would be violent clashes between the two races as a result of the "natural" hatred between blacks and whites.

"Colored only" signs were common in the segregated South. This sign points to a "Colored Waiting Room" at a Greyhound bus station in Rome, Georgia.

In a 1908 case, *Berea College* v. *Kentucky*, the Supreme Court again allowed state segregation laws to stand. The case involved Berea College, a private institution that had taught black and white students for decades. The state of Kentucky required the private college to segregate after passage of a law in 1904 that banned racially mixed schools. The lawyers presenting Kentucky's case maintained that blacks were not as intelligent as whites and that those of mixed race were even less intelligent. The state passed the law, they said, "to maintain the purity of blood." If blacks and whites were allowed to mingle, they might decide to have children together, which, according to the lawyers, would be "detrimental to the public peace and morals." The Court ruled that the state had the right to regulate the college. Again, Justice Harlan dissented, to no avail.

The Court's failure to take a stand against segregation encouraged states to extend racial separation to all aspects of life. Restaurants, bars, and hotels barred blacks from entering. Sports events and theaters played to segregated audiences. State officials enforced laws that required blacks to use separate restrooms, water fountains, and store entrances. Even in court, black witnesses swore to tell the truth on Bibles set aside for blacks only.

ᴡᴀʀs ʙʀɪɴɢ ᴄʜᴀɴɢᴇ

In the following decades, however, upheaval caused by two world wars and a devastating Depression would change society and the role black citizens played in it. More than 350,000 black Americans served in the military in segregated units in World War I. In France, 171 black soldiers received the French Legion of Honor in recognition of their bravery. Many of these same soldiers returned to America to be treated as second-class citizens. Tensions that had been simmering between blacks and whites reached the boiling point. Race riots erupted in Northern cities for the first time.

The Great Depression brought both hope and despair to black Americans. Already among the poorest citizens, blacks struggled to survive in the economic chaos of the 1930s. Southern states passed new laws to prevent blacks from voting in primary elections. Without power, blacks had no influence on politicians and no say in local government.

The election of Franklin D. Roosevelt as president in

1932 opened doors to black citizens. Roosevelt's New Deal legislation set up literacy programs that taught more than 100,000 black adults to read and write. The Civilian Conservation Corps provided jobs for 250,000 workers.

Japan's attack on Pearl Harbor on December 7, 1941, thrust the nation into World War II. More than one million blacks served in the armed forces during the war. Another million or so worked in plants manufacturing weapons and military equipment, where they learned new skills and earned decent wages. At first, the plants were segregated. But in 1941 labor leader A. Philip Randolph threatened to bring tens of thousands of black protesters to Washington, D.C., if the plants were not desegregated. To avoid the march, President Roosevelt ordered that government and defense industry workers not be discriminated against "because of race, creed, color, or national origin." In addition, Roosevelt set up the Committee on Fair Employment Practices to oversee complaints.

At war's end, President Harry Truman ordered the armed forces to desegregate. He also appointed blacks to high government offices and desegregated federal civil service jobs.

Americans entered the 1950s focused on building homes in the spreading suburbs, raising families, and getting back to normal after the disruptions of World War II. Black soldiers returning from war shared in these dreams of a better life. The GI bill paid college costs for black soldiers as well as white. A healthy economy raised incomes and helped expand the ranks of a black middle class. With their contributions, the NAACP grew in influence and prestige. Black leaders in the North and the South began to demand changes in a system that treated their people as second-class citizens. Improving education for black children lay at the center of these efforts.

THree
SEPARATE BUT NOT EQUAL

THE FIRST SUCCESSFUL BATTLES to desegregate the schools began in the colleges of the South. From Reconstruction to the 1950s, Southern black students who wanted to attend college went to all-black schools or to schools in the North. Southern states sent the few black graduate students to Northern universities. For Lloyd Lionel Gaines, that wouldn't do. He planned to become a lawyer and practice law in his home state of Missouri. The University of Missouri's law school would be the best place to study the state's legal system. He applied to the school in 1935 and was rejected. The state offered to send him to a law school in Kansas, Nebraska, Iowa, or Illinois. Missouri had no law school for blacks.

Gaines's suit against the university's registrar, S. W. Canada, made its way to the Supreme Court. Membership on the Court had shifted since the *Plessy* case, and black civil rights supporters hoped a ruling would favor their cause. In 1938, the Court ruled in Gaines's favor. The ruling upheld the "separate but equal" doctrine set forth in *Plessy*. But it said that Gaines was entitled to equal treatment under the law, as guaranteed by the Fourteenth Amendment. If the state provided a black law school equal to that available to white students, the Court would allow segregation. Otherwise, the all-white law school would have to admit black students.

LLOYD LIONEL Gaines: Opening the door to advanced education

In 1935, after graduating with honors from Lincoln University, Lloyd Lionel Gaines applied to the law school at the University of Missouri in Columbia. The state university accepted only white students. He wrote a note to the president of Lincoln University, saying he was applying for admission to the law school "with no other hope than this initial move will ultimately rebound to increase the opportunities for intellectual advancement of the Negro youth."

When university registrar S. W. Canada learned that Gaines was black, he sent the young man a telegram advising him to confer with the Lincoln University president "regarding possible arrangements and further advice." The president advised Gaines to accept the state's offer to pay tuition at a law school in a neighboring state where black students were allowed to attend. Instead Gaines informed the University of Missouri that he preferred to attend the state's law school. University officials ignored his request and took no action on his application for admission.

At the same time, National Association for the Advancement of Colored People (NAACP) lawyer Charles H. Houston, a prominent black civil rights lawyer educated at Harvard School of Law, had begun searching for cases to challenge the lack of educational opportunities for black students in the South. Houston took on Gaines's case.

In January 1936, Houston filed suit in Boone County Circuit Court in Columbia, Missouri, asking that the university either accept or reject Gaines's application. The following month the university board voted to reject Gaines's application because he was black.

Houston filed a new suit, *Gaines* v. *Canada*, claiming that the rejection "solely on the basis of color was a clear violation of the Fourteenth Amendment to the U. S. Constitution."

A crowd of about two hundred gathered for the trial on a hot summer day in July 1936. Blacks and whites sat next to each other in the packed courthouse as Houston and other lawyers argued the *Gaines* case. (The Boone County courtroom was not segregated, and neither were its restrooms or water fountains.)

Gaines, now twenty-four, sat next to his lawyers at the plaintiff's table in the front of the court. The fact that two black men had recently been lynched in the Columbia area added to the tension in the sweltering room.

In his testimony before the court, Gaines said he wished to practice law. He told the court that even with the state paying tuition fees, it would cost him more to attend school far from home. He also argued that Missouri's law school provided a better education in Missouri state law than any school outside the state. In addition, he noted that lawyers who graduated from the local law school would have connections and familiarity with the local courts that lawyers from out-of-state schools would not have. Gaines denied that he had filed suit at the suggestion of the NAACP.

The university's lawyers argued that if Gaines did not want to attend an out-of-state law school, he should petition the all-black Lincoln University to set up a law school for African Americans. He had no claim, they contended, to attend the all-white Missouri law school.

Under Houston's cross-examination, registrar Canada acknowledged that the university had enrolled non-white students of Asian ethnicity. He testified that the only students barred because of race were of African descent. The president of the university predicted that Gaines's admission to the school "would create a great amount of trouble," although he admitted he had not talked with officials in other state universities that allowed black students to attend with white students.

Two weeks after the trial, the circuit court judge denied Gaines's request, and the case went to the state supreme court. When that court also ruled against Gaines, the NAACP appealed the case to the U.S. Supreme Court.

On December 12, 1938, Chief Justice Charles Evans Hughes announced the Court's six-to-two decision in favor of Gaines. (The one vacant seat on the Court had not yet been filled.) In his majority opinion, Hughes wrote that Missouri had violated Gaines's right to the equal protection of the laws guaranteed in the Fourteenth Amendment. Gaines was entitled, Hughes said, to have Missouri "furnish within its borders facilities for legal education substantially equal to those which the State afforded for persons of the white race, whether or not other Negroes sought the same opportunity."

To some black observers, the decision was "the greatest victory Negroes had won since freedom." Houston noted that the ruling reversed policy in sixteen states where black students were barred from attending all-white colleges and universities.

Gaines was working for the civil service department in Lansing, Michigan, when the court announced its decision in his case. He said he would seek advice from his lawyers before making any plans.

Some white students at the law school warned that Gaines would be "treated like a dog" if he attended classes. Others said they would withdraw from the university rather than go to school with a black student. The student newspaper, however, promoted racial equality and called for classmates to "pioneer the nation out of this last frontier of racial prejudice and superstition."

Despite the ruling, Missouri continued its efforts to

bar Gaines's admission. Instead of allowing Gaines to attend the University of Missouri's law school, legislators passed—by a wide margin—a bill ordering Lincoln University to build a law school for black students. But the legislation vastly underfunded the project, and black leaders denounced it as yet another way to avoid desegregation.

On September 21, 1939, Lincoln University's new law school welcomed thirty black students. Gaines did not show up for classes. The law school had four instructors, ten thousand books in its library, and a dean from Howard University. Classes were held in a rented building in St. Louis. On opening day, a group of black activists and their sympathizers picketed the school in protest.

The NAACP filed suit in circuit court to determine if Missouri's establishment of the Lincoln law school met the Supreme Court's requirements. In October 1939, Charles Houston took depositions from the Lincoln instructors to prepare for the hearing. When Houston sought testimony from Gaines, the prospective law student could not be found.

Gaines had left his job in Michigan and returned to St. Louis at the end of 1938. According to his friends, the young man had intended to attend the law school in the fall. In January 1939 he told a group at the NAACP in St. Louis that he was "ready, willing, and able to enroll in the law department of the University, and had the fullest intention of doing so." But his mother said later that she didn't think her son planned to attend the school and that she thought it was too dangerous.

Sometime in early 1939, Gaines left St. Louis to speak to a group in Kansas City. In March he wrote a letter to his mother telling her he was looking for work in Chicago. After he ran out of money, fraternity brothers at the Alpha Phi Alpha house in Chicago let him stay there. A few days later he sent his mother a postcard. She said that Gaines had written, "Goodbye, if you don't hear from me anymore, you'll know I'll be all right." It was the last time she ever heard from him.

One evening in mid-March, Gaines walked out of the fraternity house, saying he was going to buy stamps. No one ever saw him again.

The NAACP tried unsuccessfully to track him down. Articles and photographs in newspapers across the country turned up nothing. What happened to Gaines? Some people thought white segregationists killed him or bribed him to stay away. Others thought he might have committed suicide or run away from the publicity.

Without Gaines to testify, the court cancelled the hearing and dismissed further proceedings in the case.

Even so, the *Gaines* case—the first education case involving black students to win in the Supreme Court—paved the way for future cases, including *Brown* v. *Board of Education*, which led to desegregation nationwide. After the Supreme Court ruled in favor of black students in the *McLaurin* and *Sweatt* cases in 1950, the University of Missouri—under court order—admitted its first black students.

One of Gaines's friends reported after his disappearance that he had told her, "If I don't go [to law school], I will have at least made it possible for some other boy or girl to go."

The doors of opportunity opened to black students thanks in large part to Gaines's willingness to fight against segregation and inequality. In 2002 the University of Missouri-Columbia named its Black Culture Center after Gaines.

As it turned out, Gaines never did attend law school. On March 19, 1939, he left the Chicago house where he was staying with friends, saying he was going out to buy stamps. He was never seen again. When he disappeared, the NAACP lawyers seeking to force Missouri to abide by the Supreme Court ruling had to drop their suit. Nevertheless, the high court's decision in the *Gaines* case pushed forward the cause of school desegregation.

MAKESHIFT SCHOOLS

Another aspiring law student, Ada Lois Sipuel, faced a similar ordeal. She applied to an all-white law school in Oklahoma in 1946. The state had begun building a law school for blacks, but it was not yet finished. Officials told Sipuel she could not enter the white school because

ADA LOIS SIPUEL FOUGHT FOR THE RIGHT TO ATTEND THE ALL-WHITE LAW SCHOOL AT THE UNIVERSITY OF OKLAHOMA. THE SCHOOL CONTENDED THAT IT WAS BUILDING A "SEPARATE BUT EQUAL" FACILITY FOR BLACK STUDENTS. THURGOOD MARSHALL (SECOND FROM LEFT) ARGUED BEFORE THE SUPREME COURT THAT SIPUEL SHOULD BE ABLE TO BEGIN HER STUDIES IN THE EXISTING SCHOOL IMMEDIATELY RATHER THAN WAIT TILL THE SCHOOL FOR BLACK STUDENTS OPENED ITS DOORS.

she was black. She would have to wait until the black law school opened its doors.

Thurgood Marshall argued her case before the Supreme Court. If white students could begin law studies immediately, Marshall told the court, his client should have an equal right to do so. The Court agreed and in 1948 ordered the law school to admit Sipuel. Instead, the state set up a separate "law school" for Sipuel. It consisted of three part-time instructors whose classroom was a roped-off section of the state capitol building.

Marshall went back to court, protesting that the state had failed to provide equal education for his client. But the Court declined to rule on the matter because the issue of equal education had not been raised in the earlier suit.

The case of Herman Marion Sweatt gave Marshall the chance he was looking for. Sweatt, a black man, applied for admission to the University of Texas School of Law at Austin in 1946. The regents refused to admit him. After a lower court ordered the school to allow Sweatt to attend, state officials set up a separate "school" for Sweatt. It resembled Oklahoma's one-person school. Held in rented rooms, the makeshift school hired two lawyers to teach Sweatt his lessons. By the time Sweatt's case reached the appeals court, the state had added a trained faculty and a library.

Nevertheless, Marshall argued that the school did not compare with that provided white students. A law-school dean testified that "it isn't enough to have a good professor. It is equally essential that there be a well-rounded, representative group of students in the classroom to participate in the . . . discussion." Sweatt received welcome support from the white students at the school. Two thousand of them attended a rally to support the cause. Many of them joined the NAACP, forming the first all-white branch in the country at that time.

Despite the strong show of support, the lower court

ruled against Sweatt. The Supreme Court heard the case, *Sweatt* v. *Painter*, on April 4, 1950. That same day the Court listened to arguments in a similar case, *McLaurin* v. *Oklahoma State Regents for Higher Education*. George W. McLaurin, a sixty-eight-year-old black retired university professor, had been turned down after he applied to the University of Oklahoma's graduate school. In 1948 the district court ordered his admission. When he got to class, though, McLaurin was forced to sit behind a railing marked "Reserved for Colored." White supporters tore down the barrier, but McLaurin still had to sit apart from his classmates. In the cafeteria he had to eat at a separate table, and he had to study in a special area set aside for him in the library. McLaurin protested his treatment to the Supreme Court.

NAACP lawyers W. J. Durham and Thurgood Marshall presented Sweatt's case to the Court. Attorney General Price Daniel and assistant Attorney General Joe R. Greenhill argued for the state of Texas. In the Oklahoma case, Robert L. Carter, special assistant counsel for the NAACP, and Amos T. Hall spoke for McLaurin. Fred Hansen, assistant attorney general of Oklahoma, represented the Oklahoma State Regents for Higher Education.

AT THE CENTER OF BATTLE
It was clear that these cases lay at the center of the battle against school segregation. North Carolina Attorney General Harry McMullan said the *Sweatt* case was "the most important to the South since Civil War days," reported the *Houston Informer*, a black newspaper covering the proceedings.

A host of interested parties presented evidence on one side or the other. Among those voicing support for desegregation was U.S. Attorney General J. Howard McGrath. During arguments in a railroad case heard just before the school cases, McGrath told the Court that the Constitution did not allow laws that segregated people by race. For the first

Though a Supreme Court ruling forced the University of Oklahoma to admit sixty-eight-year-old retired professor George W. McLaurin to its graduate school, he was forced to sit behind a railing marked "Reserved for Colored" while attending his first class in 1948. The students pulled down the railing, but he still had to sit separately.

time, the government attacked *Plessy*'s "separate but equal" doctrine and asked the Court to reverse the decision. Even if blacks and whites had equal facilities, McGrath argued, segregation "is in itself discriminatory." Unless America ended the practice, he said, segregation would strike a serious blow "at our democracy before the world."

The federal government also took a strong stand against segregation in its briefs supporting both Sweatt and McLaurin. Others arguing for desegregation included national teachers' associations, veterans' groups, and civil rights organizations.

Texas had marshalled support from eleven Southern states. Arkansas, Florida, Georgia, Kentucky, Louisiana, Mississippi, North Carolina, Oklahoma, South Carolina, Tennessee, and Virginia filed briefs in the *Sweatt* case defending Texas's actions and supporting segregation.

Attorney Carter led off the arguments for McLaurin. He contended that black students had to endure "undue hardships" because of the state's segregation policies. "Our position," Carter said, "is that no state has a right to make such a law."

Assistant Attorney General Hansen, presenting Oklahoma's case, predicted that black colleges would be forced to close and violence would erupt if the state was forced to desegregate its university. "Our white and Negro schools will fall, and trouble will be all over, great trouble," he told the Court. "Segregation isn't based solely on color alone," he added, "but for public interests." He argued further that such an action would put 1,600 black teachers out of work because the white schools would not hire them.

"It may be that in ten years," Hansen conceded, "they [blacks and whites] will all be in the same school, but now we have to do only as we find the public will stand for it." He did not know then that the order to desegregate all public schools would come just four years later. It would take much longer, however, for schools to fulfill the Court's order.

Attorney Hall disputed Hansen's claim that segregation was necessary to keep the peace. Marshall then took his turn before the justices to argue the *Sweatt* case. The plain words of his opening statements left no doubt about his views: The Court should use this case to rule that segregation was unconstitutional.

Marshall said,

> I want this court to know, that I don't care how equal those schools are, if they were exact duplicates, with the same faculty and to the ounce in cement. They are segregated and cannot be equal in any sense of the word. . . . We want governmentally enforced segregation destroyed.

TWO unanimous RULINGS

On June 5, 1950, Chief Justice Fred M. Vinson delivered two unanimous decisions in the *Sweatt* and *McLaurin* cases. The Court ruled in favor of both plaintiffs. But the justices skirted around the core issue: whether segregation was constitutional. For the moment, at least, *Plessy*'s "separate but equal" doctrine would remain the law of the land.

Even so, there was room for celebration in the two decisions. Both rulings made it clear that "separate but equal" facilities had to be equal as well as separate. In the *Sweatt* decision, the Court noted that the black law school set up by Texas may have had a good faculty and an extensive library, but it could not compete with the University of Texas in "the reputation of the faculty, experience of the administration, position and influence of the alumni, standing in the community, traditions and prestige."

In addition, the ruling noted, black students at the makeshift schools were separated from white members of the society, who made up 85 percent of the population. Segregation kept the black student from associating with key members of the legal system: judges, lawyers, jurors, and other court officials. This, the Court said, was a clear violation of the equal protection clause of the Fourteenth Amendment. As a result, the justices ordered Texas to admit Sweatt to the University of Texas Law School on equal terms with white students.

Likewise, the Court ordered the Oklahoma regents to do away with the barriers erected between McLaurin and other students. "Such restrictions," read the decision, "impair and inhibit his ability to study, to engage in discussions and exchange views with other students, and, in general, to learn his profession."

The two decisions left no doubt that states would now have to open the doors of their universities to black students. The bigger question—the inherent inequality of segregation itself—would be left for another day.

four
Through the Court System

THURGOOD MARSHALL AND THE NAACP now focused their attention on the five school cases making their way through the court system. Convinced that segregation was unjust, they planned to use these cases to prove it. Ultimately, they intended to convince the Supreme Court to overturn *Plessy* and order an end to segregation in public education.

The district court heard the first of the six crucial cases, *Bolling* v. *Sharpe*, in 1951. Attorney James Nabrit Jr. told the court that Spottswood Bolling Jr. and his classmates should be allowed to attend the all-white school in their Washington, D.C., neighborhood. He based his claim on the Fifth Amendment's guarantee that "No person shall . . . be deprived of life, liberty, or property without due process of law." In making his point, Nabrit cited a 1923 Supreme Court case called *Meyer* v. *Nebraska*. The ruling in the case said that the Fifth Amendment guaranteed "the right of the individual to acquire useful knowledge" and that this right was "not to be interfered with . . . by legislative action which is arbitrary."

Segregation, Nabrit contended, was arbitrary and unjust. He asked the court to end it. The district court rejected Nabrit's arguments in April 1951. The lawyer began working on an appeal as the other school cases took their turn in court.

MIXED MESSAGE

Early in 1951, the South Carolina legislature approved a three-cent sales tax to pay for new schools for black students. It was an attempt to keep in place the state's segregated schools by heading off the NAACP's claims of inequality. In addition, South Carolina legislators became the first in the nation to set up an official committee to fight desegregation. Among its actions, the committee blocked state aid for schools that accepted both black and white students.

The *Briggs* case proceeded despite the state's maneuvers. On May 28, 1951, NAACP lawyers appeared before a three-judge federal panel in South Carolina on behalf of Harry Briggs and the other plaintiffs. Robert Figg, the prosecuting attorney, represented the state of South Carolina in the case. Figg began by pointing out the legislature's efforts to upgrade black schools. He argued that the case should be halted to give South Carolina time to make amends.

Thurgood Marshall questioned whether the state could correct the problem. He estimated it would take $40 million to make the black schools equal to those attended by white children. And that wasn't the only injustice, the lawyers told the court. The NAACP's Carter, now working with Marshall on *Briggs*, presented studies that showed segregation in the schools caused psychological harm to black students.

Figg cited *Plessy*'s "separate but equal" doctrine to support his arguments. He also noted that Congress had approved segregation in the capital city's schools. He hinted that South Carolina might refuse to collect taxes for schools if the court ordered the state to desegregate them.

The court sent a mixed message in a split decision issued three weeks later. John J. Parker, the presiding

THROUGH THE
COURT SYSTEM

First Stop: State Court
Almost all cases (about 95 percent) start in state courts.
These courts go by various names, depending on the
state in which they operate: circuit, district, municipal,
county, or superior. The case is tried and decided by a
judge, a panel of judges, or a jury.

The side that loses can then appeal to the next level.

First Stop: Federal Court
U.S. DISTRICT COURT—About 5 percent of cases begin
their journey in federal court. Most of these cases con-
cern federal laws, the U.S. Constitution, or disputes
that involve two or more states. They are heard in one of
the ninety-four U.S. district courts in the nation.

U.S. COURT OF INTERNATIONAL TRADE—Federal court cases
involving international trade are heard in the U.S.
Court of International Trade.

U.S. CLAIMS COURT—The U.S. Claims Court hears federal
cases that involve more than $10,000; Indian claims; and
some disputes with government contractors.

The loser in federal court can appeal to the next level.

Appeals: State Cases
Forty states have appeals courts that hear cases which have
come from the state courts. In states without an appeals
court, the case goes directly to the state supreme court.

Appeals: Federal Cases
U.S. Circuit Court—Cases appealed from U.S. district
courts go to U.S. Circuit Courts of Appeals. There are

twelve circuit courts that handle cases from throughout the nation. Each district court and every state and territory is assigned to one of the twelve circuits. Appeals in a few state cases—those that deal with rights guaranteed by the U.S. Constitution—are also heard in this court.

U.S. COURT OF APPEALS—Cases appealed from the U.S. Court of International Trade and the U.S. Claims Court are heard by the U.S. Court of Appeals for the Federal Circuit. Among the cases heard in this court are those involving patents and minor claims against the federal government.

Further Appeals: State Supreme Court
Cases appealed from state appeals courts go to the highest courts in the state—usually called supreme courts. In New York, the state's highest court is called the court of appeals. Most state cases do not go beyond this point.

Final Appeals: U.S. Supreme Court
The Supreme Court is the highest court in the country. Its decision on a case is the final word. The Court decides issues that can affect every person in the nation. It has decided cases on slavery, abortion, school segregation, and many other important issues.

The Court selects the cases it will hear—usually around one hundred each year. Four of the nine justices must vote to consider a case in order for it to be heard. Almost all cases have been appealed from the lower courts (either state or federal).

Most people seeking a decision from the Court submit a petition for *certiorari*. Certiorari means that the case will be moved from a lower court to a higher court for review. The Court receives about seven thousand of these requests annually. The petition outlines the case and gives reasons why the Court should review it.

In rare cases, for example, *New York Times* v. *United States*, an issue must be decided immediately. When a case is deemed of national importance, the Court allows it to bypass the usual lower court system and hears the case directly.

To win a spot on the Court's docket, a case must fall within one of the following categories:

- Disputes between states and the federal government or between two or more states. It also reviews cases involving ambassadors, consuls, and foreign ministers.

- Appeals from a state court that has ruled on a federal question.

- Appeals from federal appeals courts (about two-thirds of all requests fall into this category).

judge, ordered the state to provide the plaintiffs with equal schools and to report back to the court in six months. But in a two-to-one ruling, the court rejected the NAACP's plea to abolish segregation. The practice of separating black and white students had long been established, Judge Parker noted. States, and not the federal government, had the power to set segregation policy as long as they met the "separate but equal" provision. "We think . . . that segregation of the races in the public schools, so long as equality of rights is preserved, is a matter of legislative policy for the several states, with which the Federal courts are powerless to interfere."

Judge Julius Waties Waring, the lone dissenter, wrote that "segregation in education can never produce equality."

Reaction to the case was explosive. DeLaine, Briggs, and plaintiff Annie Gibson all were fired from their jobs as punishment for their stand. After DeLaine left town, his house was burned to the ground, and Gibson's husband lost land that had been in his family for generations. Julius Waring, the dissenting federal judge, fled the state after threats and censure from the South Carolina House of Representatives. DeLaine and his family also fled to New York after shots were fired into the house where they were living at the time. The local police charged DeLaine with assault after he shot back. Briggs had to move to Florida to find a job. For years he lived there and sent money home to his family in South Carolina. "It was really sad for my family," said his wife, Eliza Briggs. "My children didn't have their daddy around. He said if it didn't help our children, it would help the rest of the children coming along."

The NAACP wanted to make sure the case would help children across America. They planned to use it to change the system. In July 1951, the lawyers appealed to the U.S. Supreme Court. They based their case, in part, on Judge Waring's dissent.

segregation is unjust

On June 25, 1951, Oliver Brown and the other Topeka parents gathered in the courtroom of the U.S. District Court for Kansas. A panel of three judges prepared to hear testimony in the case.

The *Brown* team did not center their arguments on inequality of school facilities. Indeed, the black school Linda attended was as good as the white schools. Instead the lawyers argued that black students forced to live with segregation were treated unjustly.

Carter led the *Brown* charge, with help from another NAACP lawyer, Jack Greenberg, and local attorneys John and Charles Scott and Charles Bledsoe. Marshall was in New York, working on other cases. Carter called in a string of expert witnesses to testify on the harm segregation caused to black students. The work of Dr. Kenneth B. Clark lay at the heart of Carter's case. Clark, an eminent psychologist and professor at Columbia, Harvard, and Howard universities, had done extensive work on the effect of segregation on children. During his studies, Clark tested the reactions of young black children to brown and white dolls. He found that the children described the white doll as "good" or "nice," while they said the brown doll was "bad." In a fact-finding report prepared for the Mid-century White House Conference on Children and Youth in 1950, Clark concluded that segregated children felt inferior and humiliated. Such feelings, Clark reported, interfered with students' learning and lowered their ambitions and morale. A number of experts testified on Clark's studies at the *Brown* trial.

Attorney Lester Goodell, representing Kansas in the case, suggested that children who went to racially mixed schools but then had to shop, work, and live segregated from whites might suffer even more. A white boy who didn't make the school football team might suffer similar strain, he noted. The expert on the stand, Michigan psychologist Wilbur Brookover, explained the difference: state laws did not require that the white boy be left off the team.

Testimony shifted to the parents and children directly involved in the case. Oliver Brown told the court how his daughter, Linda, had to walk along the railway yard to get to her school. Other parents testified, as did a young girl who described the overcrowded school bus. The last to testify was Silas Hardrick Fleming, whose two sons attended a black school twelve blocks from their East Topeka home, while there was a white school only two blocks away. Fleming said he had agreed to join the suit "whole soul and

DR. KENNETH B. CLARK, AN EMINENT PROFESSOR AT COLUMBIA, HARVARD, AND HOWARD UNIVERSITIES, DID GROUNDBREAKING RESEARCH ON THE FEELINGS OF INFERIORITY SHOWN BY BLACK CHILDREN IN SEGREGATED SCHOOLS. HIS FINDINGS WERE KEY TO THE *Brown* DECISION.

body" because "the entire colored race is craving light, and the only way to reach the light is to start our children together in their infancy and they come up together."

The NAACP team cited the *McLaurin* and *Sweatt* decisions in calling for desegregation in elementary and high schools.

Five weeks later, Judge Walter Huxman issued the unanimous decision of the court. The panel ruled against the plaintiffs. The judges found that Topeka's black schools were comparable to those attended by whites. They also noted that the Supreme Court's *McLaurin* and *Sweatt* rulings applied to colleges, not to the lower grades. With *Plessy* still intact, the lower court was forced to allow segregation.

Huxman did, however, attach several findings of fact to

the opinion in support of the NAACP claim that segregation harmed students. Among the findings was the following:

> Segregation of white and colored children in public schools has a detrimental effect upon the colored children. The impact is greater when it has the sanction of the law; for the policy of separating the races is usually interpreted as denoting the inferiority of the Negro group. A sense of inferiority affects the motivation of a child to learn.

Commenting on the case years later, Judge Huxman said, "We weren't in sympathy with the decision we rendered. If it weren't for *Plessy* v. *Ferguson*, we surely would have found the law unconstitutional. But there was no way around it—the Supreme Court had to overrule itself."

That was exactly what the NAACP and Carter intended to convince the Court to do. They filed their appeal in the *Brown* case on September 28, 1951. The next battle, they hoped, would be fought before the Supreme Court.

A victory and a defeat

Two other school segregation cases waited to be heard in Delaware. NAACP lawyers prepared to present their arguments in *Belton* v. *Gebhart* and *Bulah* v. *Gebhart*. The two cases were joined into one because they were so similar. At the request of the state, the case was tried before the Delaware Court of Chancery. Chancellor Collins Seitz, who the year before had ordered the University of Delaware to admit black students, presided.

The trial began in October 1951. Delaware lawyer Louis Redding and the NAACP's Jack Greenberg aimed to prove that segregation put black students at a disadvantage. For this, they relied on much of the same social science research used in the Kansas case. They also maintained that the schools their clients attended were inferior to white schools in the area. On the stand, psychiatrist Frederic Wertham described his studies with both black and white children. He concluded that segregation itself—regardless of the condition of the schools or the quality of education—damaged children. "Most of the children we have examined interpret segregation in one way and only one way—and that is they interpret it as punishment," he told the court.

Witnesses described the poor conditions at the black schools and the lack of bus service. Chancellor Seitz toured the schools himself. He noted the beautiful landscaping, the fully equipped classrooms, and the extra classes offered at the white schools. The black schools, however, presented a completely different picture: no landscaping, unsanitary conditions, and no extras.

The state's lawyers defended segregation, reminding the court that Delaware law required black and white students to be separated. The U.S. Supreme Court, they said, had already ruled in *Plessy* that segregation was not unconstitutional. During testimony, state schools superintendent George Miller Jr. acknowledged that the black schools were not equal to those reserved for white students in the state. But, he said, the state was in the process of upgrading the black schools. In July 1951, the legislature had passed a law requiring the same amount be spent on each student, black or white.

Chancellor Seitz delivered his opinion in April 1952. His ruling, in favor of the plaintiffs, stunned the nation. Seitz ordered the state to admit the black students to white schools immediately. For the first time, an American court had ordered a public school to desegregate. The students, the chancellor noted, should not have to wait until the state upgraded black schools. They were entitled to equal education now. "To postpone such relief is to deny relief," Seitz wrote in his opinion. "If this be a harsh test, then I answer that a State which divides its citizens should pay the price."

Although Seitz did not rule against segregation, his thoughts on the subject were clear. "I believe the 'separate but equal' doctrine in education should be rejected," he wrote, "but I also believe its rejection must come from [the Supreme] Court."

The state appealed the decision to the Delaware Supreme Court. On August 28, 1952, that court upheld Chancellor Seitz's ruling. This time the state would be the one to appeal to the U.S. Supreme Court.

Seitz's opinion gave the NAACP and its supporters the first real victory in the war against public school segregation. But they had little time to celebrate. The fifth state school segregation case, *Davis* v. *County School Board of Prince Edward County*, had reached U.S. District Court in Richmond in February 1952. This time the state of Virginia had its own experts ready to refute the NAACP's psychological testimony.

Spottswood Robinson opened the arguments for the plaintiffs. He asked the court to void the clause in Virginia's constitution that required separate schools for black and white students. He also requested that the black school be ruled inferior to those provided for the county's white students. Robinson and NAACP lawyers Oliver Hill and Robert Carter documented the inequalities at Moton High School. Their expert witnesses once again testified to the harm caused by segregation.

Justin Moore, Virginia's lawyer, admitted that Moton didn't meet the standards of the local white high school. But he stressed the state's intention of building a new school for blacks in the county. Then Moore attacked the NAACP's case against segregation. Several witnesses defended segregation as part of Virginia's culture. The president of the University of Virginia told the court that if segregation were abolished, the white majority would no longer be willing to pay for the state's school system. The state's chief witness, a psychologist from Columbia University, disputed the NAACP's experts and dismissed their findings.

The three-judge panel returned their unanimous verdict the week after the trial ended. Unsurprisingly, the decision, written by Judge Albert Bryan, favored the state of Virginia. The court found the Moton school had inferior facilities, curricula, and bus service. But, the judges ruled, the state was acting in good faith to improve the black school.

The court's findings on segregation were even more clear-cut. Segregation, Bryan wrote, was "one of the ways of life in Virginia." This cultural reason and not prejudice was "indisputably" behind the state's requirement that black children be separated from white. Bryan noted that Virginia's constitution required segregation only in one place—public schools. That proved, he said, the importance Virginians placed on school segregation.

Judge Bryan gave no more weight to the NAACP's expert testimony than to that offered by the state's witnesses. Citing *Plessy*, he noted that it wasn't the lower court's role to rule on segregation. In dismissing the plaintiff's request to abolish segregation, he wrote, "We have found no hurt or harm to either race."

The court required only that the state "pursue with diligence and dispatch their present program" of building a new high school for the county's black students. There was no mention of a deadline.

Here was one more case for the NAACP to appeal to the Supreme Court.

FIVE
TO THE SUPREME COURT

THE SUPREME COURT IS the highest court in the United States. Its decision on a case becomes the law of the land. Each year the Court receives thousands of requests to hear cases. The justices hear only a small fraction of those.

Usually attorneys who want the Supreme Court to hear their case file a writ of certiorari with the Court. This means that the lawyers petition the Court to move the case from a lower court to the high Court for review. For a case to get a hearing, at least four justices must approve the action. To win a spot on the Court's docket, a case must generally involve one of three issues: constitutional rights or questions, a state court's ruling on a federal law, or conflicting rulings by two different courts.

Once a case is chosen, lawyers for both sides must submit briefs. These legal documents contain the arguments to support their case. The lawyers cite other cases that support their view and answer charges made by the opposing lawyers. Organizations that support one side or the other can also submit briefs outlining their views. These groups are called *amicus curiae*, meaning "friend of the court."

After the justices have reviewed the briefs, they schedule oral arguments. Lawyers for both sides present their case to the Court and answer the justices' questions. Sometimes the *amicus curiae* may also present their views. After listening to the arguments, the justices discuss the case among themselves and finally vote on it.

The Court is reluctant to overturn a previous Supreme Court decision. In most cases the justices base their opinions on past rulings. Only in extreme circumstances do the justices reverse an earlier decision.

A ruling requires only a simple majority—five of the nine justices. But in controversial cases, dissents filed by opposing justices can make it more difficult to settle the matter in the public's view. That is why the chief justice often pushes for a unanimous decision in big cases.

A DIVIDED COURT

Wide divisions existed in the U.S. Supreme Court of the 1950s. In the year before the *Brown* hearing, the justices had issued unanimous decisions in 20 percent of the cases before the Court.

Three factions vied for control. Chief Justice Fred M. Vinson led the pro-government wing of the Court. Four justices—Harold H. Burton, Stanley F. Reed, Sherman Minton, and Tom C. Clark—shared Vinson's views. These justices believed the growing power of communist nations threatened the United States. Because of this threat, they generally favored federal interests in the cases that reached the Court.

Justices Hugo L. Black and William O. Douglas took an opposite stance. They believed a too-powerful federal government posed a threat to citizens' freedoms. They viewed civil liberties as being of primary importance.

Justices Felix Frankfurter and Robert H. Jackson held the middle ground. They believed the Court should not be involved in creating new laws. Congress should make the laws, they thought; the Court's role was only to rule on whether legislation met the Constitution's standards.

All the justices agreed on one thing, however; they knew that they would soon have to confront the issue of segregation in public schools. They knew, too, that the case would be controversial. In June 1952, the justices voted to schedule arguments in the *Briggs* and *Brown* cases for late October. Just before the scheduled date, the Court postponed the arguments until December, after the 1952 presidential elections. The justices also agreed to hear the *Davis* case on the same date. By the time the arguments were to begin, the Court had also put the Washington, D.C., and Delaware cases on the docket. Justice Clark later said the Court consolidated the cases because the justices did not want the issue to "smack of being a purely southern one."

BEFORE THE SUPREME COURT

On Tuesday, December 9, 1952, Robert Carter opened arguments in the first of the school segregation cases, *Brown* v. *Board of Education of Topeka, Kansas*. Standing in the courtroom before the solemn black-robed justices, Carter based his case on the Fourteenth Amendment. "No state," he said, "has any authority under the equal protection clause of the Fourteenth Amendment to use race as a factor in affording educational opportunities among its citizens."

His client suffered harm not from inferior school buildings, Carter said, but from segregation itself. He detailed how segregation placed the black students of Topeka in "an inferior caste . . . lowered their level of aspiration . . . instilled feelings of insecurity and inferiority with them, and . . . retarded their mental and educational development." Thirty-five prominent social scientists had signed affidavits supporting the research Carter quoted.

The *Brown* case was of such interest that people waited in long lines outside the Supreme Court building for the opportunity to hear the lawyers argue the case.

Carter also argued that *Plessy* v. *Ferguson* did not apply to racial discrimination in the public schools. Instead, he said, the Court's decisions in *Sweatt* and *McLaurin* regarding colleges should logically extend to public schools as well. Segregation, Carter contended, should not be allowed to interfere with education, whether in college or in the lower grades.

But if the justices decided *Plessy* did apply to the Kansas case, Carter said, then the Court should reconsider the 1896 decision. "In our view," he said, "the 'separate but equal' doctrine should be overruled."

Paul Wilson, speaking for Kansas, defended the state law that allowed school segregation. He said:

We have never at any time entertained any doubt about the constitutionality of our statute. We think the question before this Court, is simply: Is the *Plessy* case . . . and the "separate but equal" doctrine still the law of this land?

He noted that state legislatures, the U.S. Congress, and dozens of courts had relied on the doctrine for more than seventy-five years.

Justice Burton asked Wilson if changes in society might have invalidated the "separate but equal" doctrine. Wilson replied that it was possible, but he did not believe such a change had occurred.

In answer to other questions, Wilson said blacks made up only a small proportion—about 4 percent—of Kansas's total population. He acknowledged that if the Court desegregated schools, it probably wouldn't have much of an impact on Kansas. But, he said, he could not predict the effect on states with larger black populations.

In closing, Wilson noted that Carter had not produced any evidence to show that the plaintiffs in *Brown* and the other cases had been psychologically harmed by the segregation policy.

A denial of equality

Later that afternoon, at 3:15 p.m., Thurgood Marshall presented the case for *Briggs*. He made a direct attack on South Carolina's law requiring school segregation. The law, he told the Court, was unconstitutional not only because it inevitably resulted in unequal facilities but also because segregation itself was "a denial of equality."

Like Carter, Marshall cited the work of social scientists on the matter. He also noted that he was not asking the Court to interfere with local matters, but only to lift state-imposed racial segregation. He urged the justices, "Leave the county school board, the county people, the district people, to work out their own solution of the problem, to assign children on any reasonable basis they want to assign them on."

Justice Frankfurter asked how school desegregation

would be achieved if the Court ordered it. "I think that nothing would be worse," Frankfurter said, "than for this Court . . . to make an abstract declaration that segregation is bad and then have it evaded by tricks."

Marshall replied that the Court's order would require school officials to divide students into districts without regard to race or color. If officials rigged districts to exclude black students, Marshall said, they could be taken to court for violating the order. He admitted it might take time for local school officials to put the new system in place. With an optimism that would later prove to be wildly overblown, Marshall said, "It might take six months to do it one place and two months to do it another place."

John W. Davis, speaking for South Carolina, focused on three arguments. First, he noted that the state had fully complied with the lower court's order and upgraded the black school. Secondly, he argued that the state had a right to classify students on the basis of race just as it classified them by age, sex, or mental abilities. Separating students into classes, he said, did not violate the Fourteenth Amendment.

In his final point, Davis said the social science research presented by Marshall had nothing to do with constitutional rights. He also questioned the worth of the work, noting that other experts presented differing views. His arguments extended into the next day's session. He concluded late that morning with a fervent plea for local control of schools.

He asked the justices:

Is it not a fact that the very strength and fiber of our federal system, is local self-government in those matters for which local action is competent? Is it not, of all the activities of government, the one which most nearly approaches the hearts and minds of people, the question of the education of their young?

Marshall ended arguments with a question of his own. How reasonable is a law that takes black people "out of the main stream of American life" solely because of their race and color?

Marshall concluded by reminding the Court that the Constitution protected the rights of minorities—even if the majority of people believed segregation should continue and even if they thought separating people of different races helped preserve law and order.

A matter of culture

On Wednesday afternoon, December 10, Spottswood Robinson opened arguments in the *Davis* case. He described the vast differences in schools for blacks and whites in Prince Edward County. The lower court, he said, had admitted that the black schools were inferior. But the court had not ordered the county to correct the situation immediately. This was an error, Robinson argued, and the Supreme Court should correct it by ordering the white schools to accept black students.

Justin Moore, lawyer for the state of Virginia, blamed the student strike for delaying the building of a new school for blacks. Citizens voted against a bond issue for the school after learning about the strike, Moore said. The money was raised later, and the school was scheduled to open in September 1953.

Segregation, Moore said, was part of Virginia's culture and history, dating back to just after the Civil War. He claimed that the state had originally adopted segregation to improve education for both races. Nothing in the Fourteenth Amendment, he argued, allowed the Court to set local policy, especially that involving the public schools. In fact, he noted, Virginia provided an impressive school system for its students, both black and white.

Robinson, in rebuttal, suggested that Virginia had more sinister reasons for segregation. Like the black codes that limited blacks' rights, segregation limited black students' educational opportunities, he said. He, like Marshall, argued that segregation itself violated the rights guaranteed by the Fourteenth Amendment.

LIBErTY FOr ALL
At 3:30 p.m. of the second day of hearings, NAACP lawyers George E. C. Hayes and James Nabrit Jr. presented the case for Spottswood Bolling Jr. and his classmates. Instead of opposing a state, as in the previous cases, the lawyers faced the Congress of the United States. Congress had overseen the segregated school system in the nation's capital for almost a century.

Hayes began arguments by noting that the law establishing Washington, D.C., schools did not directly require segregation. Administrators set up separate schools for blacks and whites because of politics, he said. It was an attempt to keep blacks as second-class citizens, Hayes said. This policy violated the Constitution when it barred Bolling and other black students from the white school, Hayes told the Court.

U.S. Attorney General James P. McGranery supported Bolling's arguments. In an *amicus curiae* brief, he quoted Secretary of State Dean Acheson's comments on the effect of racial discrimination on foreign affairs. Washington, D.C., Acheson wrote, "is the window through which the world looks into our house." Foreign nations, he said, disapprove of school segregation. "Other peoples cannot understand how such a practice can exist in a country which professes to be a staunch supporter of freedom, justice, and democracy." The brief urged the Court to overrule the "separate but equal" doctrine and to order schools to desegregate.

Milton Korman, representing Washington school officials, took his turn before the Court. Congress, he said, set up black schools to elevate newly freed slaves, not to subjugate them. He quoted prominent black educators, who in 1906 supported Congress's reorganization of the schools for blacks and whites.

Separating black and white students should continue, Korman argued, to preserve the peace. He noted that racial strife had erupted in Northern cities where blacks and whites attended the same school. These outbursts, Korman said, interfered with the schooling of all students. Quoting from the attorney general's brief, Korman predicted that "vexing problems . . . may arise in eliminating segregation." And, he noted, the U.S. brief also advised that desegregation be done gradually.

Nabrit ended with a stirring rebuttal to Korman's arguments. "You either have liberty or you do not," Nabrit said. "When liberty is interfered with by the state, it has to be justified, and you cannot justify it by saying that we only took a little liberty. . . . In the capital of the free world, there is no place for a segregated school system. This country cannot afford it, and the Constitution does not permit it, and the statutes of Congress do not authorize it."

Final Words

On the afternoon of the third day of arguments, the Court heard the final school segregation case, *Gebhart* v. *Belton* and *Bulah*. Unlike the other cases, this one had been appealed by the state. H. Albert Young, Delaware's attorney general, began the arguments. Noting the difficulty of presenting the last case after eight hours of arguments, Young nevertheless argued strongly against desegregation. Delaware, he said, had already begun improving black schools. Therefore, he argued, black students had no need to attend schools for whites.

The lower court's order to desegregate schools, Young told the Court, had "a terrific impact" on the entire state. Schools all over Delaware, he said, could be sued because of the order.

Arguing for *Belton* and *Bulah*, lawyers Louis Redding and Jack Greenberg asked the Court to affirm the lower court's decision. But they also asked that the high Court rule against school segregation. Otherwise, the lawyers noted, black students in Delaware would be forced back to black schools as soon as the school facilities were made equal.

Greenberg noted that his clients had been admitted to white schools and there had been no problems. He urged the Court to allow the black students to stay in the schools.

With that, the Court adjourned.

Deliberations

The Saturday after the last arguments, the justices met in the conference room behind the Court chamber. No one else was allowed in the room. As the nation waited, the justices shared their views on the *Brown* cases.

Chief Justice Vinson spoke first. He said he could not support desegregation yet. Congress, he pointed out, had not outlawed the practice. The South threatened rebellion. He suggested the Court postpone a decision on segregation until the states had a chance to upgrade black schools.

Justice Black, the next to speak, had been a supporter of Franklin Roosevelt's New Deal. A Southerner, Black had once belonged to the Ku Klux Klan, but had renounced the group's violent ways. As a Supreme Court justice, Black had

CHIEF JUSTICE FRED M. VINSON WAS NOT IN FAVOR OF SCHOOL DESEGRE-
GATION AT THE TIME THE *BROWN* CASE FIRST CAME TO COURT. HE DIED,
HOWEVER, BEFORE THE FINAL DECISION WAS RENDERED.

always supported individual rights. He continued to support them now by arguing for desegregation.

Justice Reed, who was from the border state of
Kentucky, did not believe segregation was discriminatory against blacks. In his view, the NAACP lawyers had
not proved that the policy was unconstitutional. Like
Vinson, he believed the best course was to let the states
improve black schools.

Justice Frankfurter saw the Supreme Court's role as
a limited one. A former professor at Harvard Law School
and an expert in constitutional law, Frankfurter believed

that it was up to the legislatures, not the Court, to change the status quo. He was an advocate of human liberty, but he weighed that against national stability and concerns for security. Not surprisingly, Frankfurter argued for restraint. He proposed that the Court postpone a decision in the case. According to his clerks, Frankfurter opposed segregation. But, they recalled, he did not want to rush into a decision that could disrupt efforts in the South to improve black schools. He urged the Court to wait until newly elected President Dwight D. Eisenhower took office and had time to review the case.

Even those outside the justices' chambers could have correctly guessed how Justice Douglas voted. Douglas had grown up poor in the state of Washington and relied on the lessons from his youth to decide cases. Always a champion for the underdog, Douglas urged an end to segregation.

Justice Jackson, like Frankfurter, argued to delay the vote. He proposed the justices discuss the cases in depth over several months before issuing a decision. A member of FDR's New Deal team, Jackson believed as Frankfurter did that the Court should not create laws.

Justice Burton believed the schools should be desegregated. He thought separate schools harmed blacks. In his view, the Court should vote to end segregation. Born in Massachusetts, Burton had settled in Ohio and had served as a U.S. senator from that state. A Republican, he was appointed by Democratic President Harry Truman to balance the Court.

Justice Clark sided with those who wanted to postpone the decision. A Texan, Clark served as U.S. attorney general before being appointed to the Supreme Court by President Truman. In a note to the Court regarding the *McLaurin* and *Sweatt* cases, Clark had written in 1950 that he did not think *Plessy* should be overruled at that time, though he supported the Court's action in the two cases. He noted that requiring desegregation in elementary and secondary schools was not necessary then and that he would vote against hearing a case that addressed the issue. "Perhaps at a later date," he wrote, "our judicial discretion will lead us to hear such a case."

The last to vote, Justice Minton agreed with the NAACP position that segregation was unconstitutional. He argued that *Plessy* could be overturned on the basis of *Sweatt* and *McLaurin*, as well as other cases. Another New Deal supporter, Minton had been appointed by President Truman just three years earlier. The justice would say later that the *Brown* case was the most important decision during his time on the Court. He joined Black, Douglas, and Burton in favor of ruling to end segregation.

Without a consensus, the Court took no action. As the term neared an end, the justices searched for a way to deal with the case. Frankfurter proposed a list of questions that lawyers on both sides of the issue would be asked to address. The Court agreed to reschedule the cases for arguments at the beginning of the new term on October 12.

A new hearing, a new chief justice

Over the summer, the lawyers scrambled to answer the Court's questions. The Justice Department, at the Court's request, also prepared oral arguments in the case. They all addressed these five questions:

1. Did the men who wrote and ratified the Fourteenth Amendment intend for it to abolish segregated schools?

2. Did they understand that Congress or the courts might interpret the amendment to end segregation in the schools?

3. Is it within the Court's power to end segregated schools based on the Fourteenth Amendment?

4. If segregated schools are found to be unconstitutional, should desegregation begin immediately or should the process be gradual?

5. What sort of decree should the Court issue and who should be in charge of working out the details?

Before the Court could meet, something happened that would change the course of history. In September, Chief Justice Vinson suffered a heart attack and died. President Eisenhower appointed Earl Warren, Republican governor of California, to fill the vacancy. Warren, a former district attorney, had earned a reputation as being tough on crime. The Republican president had little enthusiasm for desegregating the schools. He had grown up in Kansas, where blacks and whites had attended separate schools for decades, and had served in a segregated military. It would be futile, the president believed, for the courts to try to change segregated schools, a tradition so entrenched in American life. Eisenhower later called Warren's nomination "the biggest damn-fool mistake I ever made."

Others, however, would disagree. Warren joined the Court in October 1953. He was to become one of its most notable chief justices. The second round of arguments in the *Brown* case, postponed until after Warren's nomination, began on December 7. The Senate did not confirm Warren as chief justice, however, until March 1, 1954, months after the formal arguments ended.

As expected, the two sides held opposing views of the Fourteenth Amendment and how it related to school segregation. The NAACP lawyers again argued that black children were not getting equal treatment.

Excluding the students from white schools, the lawyers said, violated the equal protection clause of the Fourteenth Amendment.

Spottswood Robinson and Thurgood Marshall presented the case on behalf of the black students. Robinson contended that the framers wrote and ratified the Fourteenth Amendment with the purpose of guaranteeing "the complete legal equality of all persons, irrespective of race." They did this, he said, with full knowledge that it would override the states' ability to discriminate on the basis of race.

John Davis, in his turn, disputed Robinson's conclusions. South Carolina's lawyer contended that neither Congress nor the state legislatures had any idea when the amendment was ratified that it would ban segregated schools. And, he argued, just because blacks and whites had to attend separate schools did not mean that blacks were treated unfairly.

The justices wrestled with another question: how to achieve desegregation at the nation's schools. Assistant Attorney General J. Lee Rankin presented the federal government's recommendations. The Court, Rankin said, should send the cases back to the lower courts with an order to desegregate the schools. School districts would be given a year to come up with a plan that met the Court's approval.

But how does the Court make districts desegregate the schools when they refuse to do so, the justices wanted to know.

"I foresee a generation of litigation if we send it back with no standards, and each case has to come here to determine it standard by standard," Justice Jackson predicted.

Rankin noted that the lower courts could handle most of the cases. The schools, in turn, would be expected to desegregate "with all diligent speed." The Court's ruling in the case, Rankin acknowledged, would affect far more than just the schools represented in the cases before the justices.

As expected, the lawyers for each side of the issue presented dramatically different scenarios. Those representing the black students wanted schools to desegregate by the following school term, September 1954. Their opponents argued for a gradual change, if one had to be made. These lawyers argued that desegregation could be accomplished much more successfully by leaving it to local communities to work out their own plans on their own schedules.

South Carolina's Davis argued passionately for states' rights and local control. "Your Honors do not sit, and cannot sit, as a glorified Board of Education for the State of South Carolina or any other state," he told the justices.

The arguments ended on December 9. The time, according to the clock hanging from the ceiling above the justices, was 2:40 p.m. After three intense days of debate, the Court adjourned. The justices once again retired to their chambers to discuss the cases that would change American schools—and lives—forever.

in conference

Justice Tom Clark once said, "You know, we don't have money at the Court for an army, and we can't take ads in the newspapers, and we don't want to go out on a picket line in our robes. We have to convince the nation by the force of our opinions."

Warren understood this. A decision backed by all the justices carried much more weight than one issued by a split Court. Opponents had something to cling to when a dissent, or even a concurring opinion, was issued. Concurring opinions support the final vote but present different reasons for doing so. In this case, especially, Warren knew that the Court needed to issue a clear, unanimous decision. He set out to get one. For the next five months, Warren used the political skills he had learned as governor to forge an agreement.

During the justices' first discussion of the case the Saturday morning after arguments ended, Warren made it clear that he favored desegregation. Segregation, he said, could no longer be justified. Justices Douglas, Black, Burton, and Minton had supported that view after the first hearings. They continued to do so.

Justice Clark also saw the need to end segregation, but as a Southerner he knew many would oppose such a step. He feared violent opposition to any ruling that required immediate action. Clark argued for a gradual approach. The South, he believed, needed time and leeway to work out the best way to desegregate schools in their area.

Justices Frankfurter and Jackson had mixed feelings about the case. They were reluctant to overturn established legal precedent. But in the end, they agreed to go along with the decision to abolish school segregation.

Finally only Reed balked at a Court order to end segregation in the nation's schools. Forcing the South to desegregate schools, he feared, would increase racial tensions and slow the strides that had been made to end discrimination.

During these months, the Court heard and decided other cases. Week after week, they continued to discuss the *Brown* cases. Near the end of February, the justices voted privately on the matter. Although eight of the justices agreed on ending segregation, they all had different ideas on the decision itself. Jackson seemed likely to write a concurring opinion. Reed, the only one to vote no, seemed committed to issuing a dissent.

Using all his skill as a mediator, Warren worked out a compromise. The entire Court would agree to a ruling ending school segregation. Warren would write the decision, which would be issued by the end of the term in June. The Court would issue a second ruling during the next term on how to desegregate the nation's schools. That way, the South would have a year to get used to the new policy.

Before Warren could write the decision, however, Jackson had a heart attack. The justices decided to go ahead with the *Brown* case anyway, since it had already been delayed so long. Warren wrote the decision and gave it to the other justices to review on May 7. At that point, the justices could decide whether to sign the majority decision or write one of their own.

When the justices met for their May 15 conference, they gave final approval to the decision. From his hospital bed, Jackson agreed, too. The decision, after years of court cases and two sessions before the Supreme Court, would be unanimous.

THE PATH TO UNANIMITY

It takes only a simple majority for a case to win a U.S. Supreme Court victory. In a full court, that means five votes to four. Controversial cases—like *Brown*—may require a stronger show of support from justices if they are to be accepted by the American public.

The justices supporting desegregation knew they would have to have a strong majority to back up any ruling ordering such a dramatic change in American education. Behind closed doors, the justices deliberated the issue, delayed a decision, and finally forged an agreement that led to a unanimous decision. Given the wide range of opinions held by the justices on the matter, the 9–0 *Brown* ruling was a testament to Chief Justice Earl Warren's abilities as a negotiator and the justices' willingness to put the good of the nation before their individual beliefs.

In deliberations after the first oral arguments in the *Brown* case in 1952, four justices—William O. Douglas, Hugo Black, Sherman Minton, and Harold Burton—took strong stands against segregated schools. They believed that segregation violated the Constitution.

Four other justices—including Chief Justice Frederick M. Vinson—were equally opposed to a ruling that would force school desegregation. Those against such a ruling believed generally that it was not the proper role of the Court to rule by decree. The ruling, they knew, would overturn practices deeply entrenched in the states' history and culture. Such an upheaval should come about through congressional action, they believed.

Like several of his colleagues, Justice Felix Frankfurter had often argued for judicial restraint in changing laws. But he also despised segregation. He urged the justices to delay their vote in the *Brown* case until both sides could reargue the case. The issue required more examination, he said, and lawyers needed to focus on the Fourteenth Amendment's meaning and intent.

The balance changed when Chief Justice Vinson died. His replacement, Earl Warren, brought a much different perspective to the bench. An opponent of school segregation, he was a consensus builder and a skilled politician. During deliberations following the second round of oral arguments in December 1953, the four original opponents of segregated schools remained firm. Justice Frankfurter turned from his neutral stance and made clear his support for school desegregation. The law, he argued, must reflect "changes in men's feelings for what is right and just."

Warren added a sixth vote to the majority. But before taking the vote, Warren set out to convince his fellow justices to unite behind the decision. The new chief justice spent hours listening to the concerns of each justice. Frankfurter, too, lobbied for a unified vote. He flooded the justices with memos outlining his reasons for supporting the change.

Justice Tom Clark, who did not like segregation, had originally thought the states should tackle the problem. But with the majority in favor of desegregated schools, Clark said he would vote to abolish segregation. In pledging support for the majority opinion, however, he told Warren, "the remedy must be carefully worked out."

Justice Jackson posed a different problem for Warren. Jackson had agreed to vote with the majority, but he seemed determined to write his own opinion on the case. Warren believed a second opinion would weaken the ruling. He urged Jackson to reconsider.

According to his law clerk, E. Barrett Prettyman Jr., Jackson drafted a twenty-three-page concurring opinion on the case. When Jackson asked what he thought of the draft, Prettyman noted that the justice had spent most of the brief defending the segregationist South, with only the last section devoted to explaining why the system had to change. The clerk told Jackson it sounded as if the justice were ashamed of the majority decision instead of supporting it. Shortly after writing his opinion, Jackson suffered a heart attack.

Meanwhile, Warren had drafted his short, to-the-point majority opinion in the Kansas case and a second in the Washington case. Fearing leaks, he hand-delivered them to the justices still at the Court and had his assistant carry them to the rest. Warren himself took copies to Jackson in the hospital. Prettyman said Jackson seemed relieved after he read the opinions. The justice told Warren he would support them. Jackson never circulated his drafted concurrence.

Warren made his final delivery to Justice Stanley Reed, now the last holdout. Raised in Kentucky, Reed knew the South and believed the Court rulings might hinder the efforts being made there to improve relations between the races. He felt strongly that the law did not support the Court's actions. Even so, Reed knew the importance of the decisions. In the end, he decided to go along with the majority for the good of the nation. In a note to Frankfurter after the decision was announced, Reed wrote: "While there were many considerations that pointed to a dissent they did not add up to a balance against the Court's opinion. . . . [T]he factors looking toward a fair treatment for Negroes are more important than the weight of history."

At a private conference on Saturday, May 15, the justices approved Earl Warren's rulings in the Kansas and D.C. cases and vowed to keep the vote secret until the official announcement the following Monday. Warren later gave credit for the unanimous decision to the three Southern justices—Black, Reed, and Clark—who voted with the majority even though they faced "animosity and harassment in [their] home states because of centuries-old patterns of life."

On May 17, Warren read the two decisions to the world. All nine Supreme Court justices, including Jackson, who had left his hospital bed to attend, were in the courtroom. Thurgood Marshall, who had argued for *Brown*, listened intently as Warren outlined the facts of the case. During the reading, Marshall stared hard at Reed, whom he expected to issue a dissent.

Warren came to the crucial words of the decision: "We conclude that in the field of public education the doctrine of 'separate but equal' has no place." Then, he inserted the word "unanimously" after "we hold," and continued, "that the plaintiffs and others . . . have been deprived of the equal protection of the laws guaranteed by the Fourteenth Amendment." The listeners in the packed courtroom gasped. Marshall nodded slightly at Reed, who nodded back. There would be no dissent.

SIX
A MOMENTOUS DECISION

AT 12:52 P.M. on Monday, May 17, 1954, Chief Justice Earl Warren began reading the Court's opinion in the *Brown* case. Alerted by the Court's press officer, reporters rushed to the courtroom where the justices and their clerks had gathered.

Well aware of the opinion's importance, the chief justice read the words that would change America. He began with a description of the cases that had been joined together to form *Brown*. As Warren detailed the cases and the role of the Fourteenth Amendment, reporters listened attentively, waiting impatiently to hear how the Court would rule on school segregation.

The plaintiffs, Warren read, claimed that segregated schools could not be made equal and should not be allowed. They based their claims on the Fourteenth Amendment's guarantee of "equal protection of the laws."

Warren noted that the lawyers in the case had explored the history of the Fourteenth Amendment during rearguments. After a thorough study of the amendment, however, the Court concluded it could not base its decision on conditions that existed when the amendment was adopted in 1868. The study, he said, proved to be "inconclusive" as far as the *Brown* case was concerned.

Warren described the sad state of public education in the 1860s. The passage of the Fourteenth Amendment,

Warren noted, had little effect on public schools of the time.

The chief justice outlined the *Plessy* v. *Ferguson* case, which established the "separate but equal" doctrine that the nation's courts had clung to for more than fifty years.

More than halfway through reading the decision, Warren noted that the black school cases involved in the *Brown* suit were either as good as corresponding white schools or were being upgraded. Because of that, Warren said, the Court based its decision not on "tangible factors" such as buildings, programs, and teacher qualifications, but on "the effect of segregation itself on public education."

The opinion detailed the importance of education in present-day life. Indeed, Warren noted, to succeed in life, a child must be educated. Because of the central role schools play in everyone's life, the opportunity for education "is a right which must be made available to all on equal terms." That said, Warren asked the key question of the *Brown* case: Does segregation on the basis of race deprive minority students of equal educational opportunities?

"We believe that it does," Warren said to the crowd of reporters and others gathered to hear the decree.

Separating black students from whites solely because of their race, Warren said, made the minority students feel inferior. That in turn, he continued, "may affect their hearts and minds in a way unlikely ever to be undone." And when laws require such segregation, Warren noted, the negative effect on students is even greater. Students treated in such a way have less motivation to learn. This conclusion, he said, was "amply supported by modern authority." In a footnote, Warren listed more than half a dozen sociological studies to back up this view.

Reading the final paragraphs of the momentous decision, Warren spoke the words that would send the reporters running for their phones and would soon embroil a nation

THE *BROWN* DECISION STRUCK DOWN LAWS ALLOWING SEGREGATION IN THE NATIONS' PUBLIC SCHOOLS. SPOTTSWOOD BOLLING, A PLAINTIFF IN THE CASE, AND HIS MOTHER, READ ABOUT THE RULING IN THE NEWSPAPER.

in controversy. The doctrine of "separate but equal," he said, had no place in public education. Segregation deprived minority students of the equal protection guaranteed them under the Fourteenth Amendment. As such, segregation in public schools was unconstitutional and would no longer be allowed under the law.

To decide the best way to desegregate the schools—a task that Warren acknowledged would be complex—the Court would hear further arguments on the matter in the fall. Warren invited attorneys general from the states where school segregation existed to present briefs on the issue by October 1, 1954.

"It is so ordered," Warren intoned, ending the reading of his first major opinion as chief justice.

Warren followed the *Brown* decision with a quick

reading of the opinion on the related *Bolling* case. In that, the Court's decision struck down segregation in public schools in the District of Columbia. The decision was based on the Fifth Amendment's guarantee to all citizens that they cannot be deprived of liberty without due process. Segregating students solely on the basis of race was unjustified, violated due process, and therefore was unconstitutional, the justices ruled.

Both opinions were unanimous.

CHanGInG HISTOrY

In less than two thousand words, Warren and the Court had changed the course of United States history. Newspapers ran the story under big headlines. "School Segregation Banned" blared the front-page story in the *Topeka State Journal*, based in the city where the case began. Almost a half century later Zelma Henderson, one of the *Brown* plaintiffs, recalled her elation at reading the story. "I felt then and I feel now that we did the right thing," she said.

Editorial writers weighed in with their opinions. In general, big-city newspapers in the North supported the opinion. In an editorial titled "All God's Chillun," *The New York Times* applauded the decision: "The highest court in the land, the guardian of our national conscience, has reaffirmed its faith—and the underlying American faith—in the equality of all men and all children before the law."

An editorial writer on the Chicago *Defender*, a newspaper that served the black community, wrote that the decision had more meaning for American democracy than the atom bomb and the hydrogen bomb. "This means the beginning of the end of the dual society in American life and the . . . segregation which supported it."

For some Southern editors, however, the opinion signaled the beginning of the end in a different way. The *Daily News* in Jackson, Mississippi, predicted "blood may stain Southern soil in many places because of this decision." The editorial angrily denounced the Court's action, saying it would lead to mixed marriages between blacks and whites and the eventual "mongrelization of the human race."

Likewise, the *Cavalier Daily*, published by the University of Virginia, said that for many Southerners, the decision "is contrary to a way of life and violates the way in which they have thought since 1619."

Few in the North realized the depths of the opposition looming over the issue. The *Times* editorial acknowledged that the desegregation required by the decision would "create problems" but suggested that Southern communities would have to adapt to new conditions. An editorial in the *Washington* (D.C.) *Post and Times Herald* predicted the decision would lead to "transient difficulties" and "irritations," but it would be viewed in the end as "profoundly healthy and healing." The effort to "close an ancient wound" would be done "speedily," the editorial writer added.

Even President Eisenhower underestimated the effect the decision would have on the nation. In a letter written to a friend in October 1954, the president predicted that the Court's orders on segregating the schools would be "very moderate." Eisenhower thought the local courts would handle most of the details. As it turned out, the president would be forced to call out federal troops to help enforce desegregation in the South.

Firestorm of Rebellion

The decision affected most directly the seventeen states (most in the South) that required school segregation, four other states whose laws allowed the practice, and Washington, D.C. The day after the Supreme Court first ruled against segregated schools, Arkansas Governor

Francis Cherry announced that his state would "comply with the requirements" of the ruling. Virginia Governor Thomas Stanley urged citizens to deal with the issue with "cool heads, calm study, and sound judgment." Alabama Governor Jim Folsom said his state would obey the ruling: "When the Supreme Court speaks," he said, "that's the law."

Because the Court had not required the schools to desegregate by a specific deadline, many state officials took a wait-and-see stance. The *Atlanta Constitution* called for Georgians to use the time before the next Court ruling to "think clearly" and "seek out construc-tive conclusions." The paper added, "It is not time to indulge demagogues on either side nor to listen to those who always are ready to incite violence and hate."

Almost immediately, though, the opinion lit a firestorm of rebellion among Southern segregationists. Many white Southerners raged that they would never allow their children to attend school with black students. Georgia's governor, Herman Talmadge, predicted "blood will run in Atlanta's streets" as a result of the decision. The day Warren issued the opinion became known as "Black Monday" in parts of the South. U.S. Senator James O. Eastland of Mississippi, South Carolina's former governor (and later U.S. Senator) Strom Thurmond, and Talmadge all pledged not to allow blacks in white schools in their states. "I do not believe in Negroes and whites associating with each other socially or in our school system, and as long as I am governor, it won't hap-pen here," Talmadge vowed. Within five weeks of the decision's reading, Virginia's governor, Thomas Stanley, had joined the segregationists. He announced, "I shall use every legal means at my command to continue segregated schools in Virginia."

In November 1954, Louisiana voters approved a state constitutional amendment that would permit school segre-gation. The following month, voters in Mississippi passed an amendment to the state constitution allowing schools to shut down to avoid desegregation.

Many Southern leaders protested that the Court had overstepped its powers. They argued that federal courts should not interfere with state operations, such as public schools. Some legal scholars attacked the Court's references to sociological studies. They contended the ruling should have been based solely on legal points. It was not the job of the Court, they argued, to interpret and act on studies, which many viewed as biased anyway.

Thurgood Marshall and other prominent black leaders celebrated the victory. But they wanted no further delays. The Court, they said, should set a deadline and order states to begin desegregation immediately.

Well aware of the potential for violence from segregationist whites, many blacks in the South did not cheer the decision. Those who did were cautious. They knew they could be fired, lose their homes, or be injured and even killed if they took a public stand for desegregation. Melba Pattillo Beals, who would later become one of nine black students to desegregate Central High School in Little Rock, Arkansas, recalled the day Justice Warren announced the *Brown* opinion. The teacher at her all-black school told the class about the Court's decision, then released the students early with a warning to be careful going home. Joyful at the unexpected time off, the twelve-year-old paid little heed as she daydreamed her way across a shortcut. A car stopped, and an angry white man jumped out and began chasing her, shouting that he would never let the likes of her go to school with his children. With help from a friend, she barely escaped being attacked.

desegregation battles

Even without a deadline, desegregation took place in many areas. Charleston, Arkansas, schools quietly admitted black students to its white schools in the fall of 1954. It was the first community in the eleven states of the Deep South to comply with the ruling to desegregate. During the 1954–1955 school year, students in Washington, D.C., Louisville, Baltimore, and St. Louis began attending racially mixed schools. High schools in Baltimore and Washington, D.C., desegregated despite attempts to block the action by two thousand white students. Junior colleges in Texas and public schools in West Virginia voluntarily accepted both black and white students. By the time Spottswood Bolling Jr. graduated, his school had become desegregated. In Topeka, the school board had voted to change its policy even before the second Supreme Court hearing.

In other areas, however, communities had no intention of desegregating without a battle. Shortly after Warren issued the *Brown* opinion, Mississippi Circuit Court Judge Tom P. Brady formed a group called the White

THOUGH MANY STATES BITTERLY OPPOSED DESEGREGATION, MANY OTHERS INTEGRATED QUIETLY. HERE, TEACHER MARJORIE BEACH TALKS TO AN INTEGRATED KINDERGARTEN CLASS IN WASHINGTON, D.C., IN SEPTEMBER 1954.

Citizens' Council. The council met for the first time in Indianola, Mississippi, two months after the *Brown* decision. The group's simple credo—that whites were superior to blacks and that the races should be separate—soon attracted members throughout the South. Weekly radio and television programs sponsored by the Citizens' Council broadcast their segregationist views.

The group spread, attracting hundreds of white business owners and other professionals in the South. Though claiming not to endorse violence, the group's members kept track of those who opposed them. In Mississippi, in particular, desegregation supporters were likely to lose their jobs or be threatened in some other way.

Perhaps surprisingly, one of the first battlegrounds over *Brown* occurred not in the South but in Delaware. In September 1954, protests erupted in the small rural community of Milford. The school board had ordered that ten black students be admitted to the town's white high school. After more than 1,500 white protesters held a noisy rally, the school board shut down the school. But when the local officials asked for state help, the state board of education refused to issue a ruling backing up the Milford board. The members of the local board resigned.

The state board took over, opening the school after a week. When the school reopened, state police officers protected the black students as they attended classes. Many of the white students refused to attend the school, and protestors continued their rallies outside the school. Small children carried signs with pro-segregation slogans. Someone burned a cross in the field across from the school. A new local school board gave in to the protesters. The board sent the black students to an all-black school twenty miles away.

With the rest of the country watching, the black students' case made its way to court. It soon became apparent that other communities would follow a similar route. In July

1954, the Board of Supervisors in Virginia's Prince Edward County passed a resolution saying the board was "unalterably opposed to the operation of nonsegregated public schools in the Commonwealth of Virginia." The board vowed to use its power to continue segregated schools.

Back at Court: *Brown II*

In working out a compromise, Chief Justice Warren had intentionally built in a cooling-off period. The Court had intended to meet after the November 1954 elections to consider how to desegregate the schools. Before that happened, Justice Jackson died. In an ironic twist, President Eisenhower appointed John Marshall Harlan to fill the vacant seat. Harlan was the grandson of Justice John Harlan, the lone dissenter in the *Plessy* case.

The appointment enraged segregationists. They viewed it as further evidence of the federal government's attempt to exert control over the states. Southern senators waged a strong fight to block Harlan's confirmation. Warren decided to wait until the ninth justice took his place on the Court before scheduling oral arguments in the followup to the *Brown* case. Harlan finally won appointment in March 1955.

By the time the Supreme Court began the second phase of the *Brown* case in April, more than half the counties in Virginia—as well as many other areas of the South—had voted to oppose desegregation in their schools.

Six states accepted the Court's invitation to present briefs in what had become known as *Brown II*. Warren had hoped the states would present ways to accomplish desegregation without too much disruption. Instead, the six states—Florida, North Carolina, Texas, Maryland, Oklahoma, and Arkansas—followed Virginia's lead in devising barriers to desegregation.

In the meantime, the federal government issued a report that disputed the South's claim that its schools were "separate but equal." According to the report, black schools would have to spend $2 billion for buses, supplies, facilities, and teachers' salaries to make black schools equal to white schools.

The Supreme Court scheduled arguments in the case to take place April 11 through 14, 1955. S. Emory Rogers, representing Clarendon County, South Carolina, led off with his views. He urged the justices to allow time for such a major change to take place. "I do not believe that in a biracial society," Rogers told the Court, "we can push the clock forward abruptly to 2015 or 2045." He asked the Court to issue a general order that did not include instructions on how or when schools must desegregate. The lower courts, he said, should oversee states' efforts to eliminate segregation in the schools.

In response to questions from Warren, Rogers acknowledged that the county would not obey the Court's decree to end segregation. "Right now we would not conform; we would not send our white children to the Negro schools," he told Warren. Those who witnessed the discussion said Warren was irate at the exchange.

Robert Figg, who had helped prepare the briefs for the state of South Carolina in the earlier case, took his turn next. He said that segregation had been part of life in the South for more than a century and was not likely to change overnight because of a court order. White parents might pull their children out of public schools altogether rather than allow them to attend with black students. He noted that despite opposition, many schools in his state had made progress toward desegregation.

Archibald Robinson argued for Virginia in the case. He gave the familiar argument that desegregation would not succeed until local attitudes changed. Schools might open to both races, he said, but citizens would nevertheless find ways to defeat desegregation. Local people, he said, "could refuse to vote the money [to run

ANGER AGAINST SUPREME COURT CHIEF JUSTICE EARL WARREN RAN HIGH LONG AFTER THE *BROWN* DECISION. HERE, A SIGN POSTED BESIDE U.S. HIGHWAY 101 IN WISCONSIN IN 1963 CALLS FOR HIS IMPEACHMENT.

schools], refuse to support necessary laws, and repeal . . . public attendance laws." A Court order, he said, would damage Virginia's school system and revive the bitterness of Southern whites during Reconstruction.

Attorneys general from Virginia and the six other Southern states warned the Court that an order to desegregate immediately would not succeed. I. Beverly Lake of North Carolina told the Court,

> Whether or not the children of this State will or will not attend public school after this year, and whether or not the people of North Carolina will or will not continue to live side by side in peace and friendliness, will depend in a large measure on the decrees about to be issued.

John Ben Shepperd, attorney general of Texas, ended the states' arguments with a plea that sounded like a demand. "It is our problem; let us solve it."

Solicitor General Simon E. Sobeloff spoke for the federal government. He backed off from a deadline but asked the Court to require desegregation "as speedily as feasible." Asked to explain "feasible," he said the Court should consider "all relevant factors" when issuing its order. But, he added, that did not mean rights guaranteed by the Constitution should depend on the results of a public opinion poll.

Sobeloff also argued against a ruling that would affect only the plaintiffs in the joined cases. If the Court followed that course, other schools would not immediately be required to desegregate. However, the decision would set a precedent, and students everywhere could bring suit to desegregate schools in their area based on the Court's ruling. "I think both sides want to have the situation settled," Sobeloff said.

WITH ALL DELIBERATE SPEED

Thurgood Marshall made the case for Brown and the other plaintiffs. In his arguments, Marshall urged the Court to order states to begin desegregation "forthwith"; in other words, immediately. There was "no justification," he said, to delay. He dismissed arguments that states would have difficulty enforcing the Court's order. "I am particularly shocked at arguments of the impotency of our government to enforce its Constitution," he told the Court.

Marshall downplayed the threat of violence referred to by several previous speakers. He noted that similar threats—but little real violence—had occurred when the courts ordered states to allow blacks to vote.

Marshall also argued that one rule should apply to all. The Constitution, he said, did not set varying standards for different parts of the country. Why should the desegregation issue, guaranteed as it was under the Fourteenth Amendment, be any different?

In the end, the Supreme Court took the path proposed by the Justice Department. Again Warren wrote and delivered the opinion. Once again, the Court unanimously backed the decision.

On May 31, 1955, Warren read the opinion to an expectant audience. He reiterated that "racial discrimination in public education is unconstitutional." Warren went on: The Court required public schools to "make a prompt and reasonable start" toward desegregation. Lower courts would oversee local efforts to achieve that goal. The courts could grant an extension if schools presented proof that they needed more time and were making a "good faith" effort to desegregate.

The Court set no deadline and no timetable. Instead, Warren used a phrase suggested by Justice Felix Frankfurter, "with all deliberate speed," rather than "forthwith" as the NAACP had proposed. The Court did not want to interfere with states' rights. By not setting a deadline or requiring schools to follow a specific plan, the justices made it easier for states to accept the Court's order. Black students would get justice, and schools would be desegregated at a pace the South could tolerate. That was the hope. As future actions would show, however, the battle had just begun.

seven
A NEW DAY

Brown II
S.C
wording
allowing
dragging
of heels

THE SECOND BROWN DECISION deeply disappointed Thurgood Marshall and the other NAACP lawyers. They believed the lack of a specific deadline would allow states to delay desegregation indefinitely. Their fears would prove to be justified.

By 1955, more white schools had opened their doors to black students. The younger sister of Linda Brown, whose father had filed the Kansas school segregation case, attended the once all-white Sumner Elementary School in Topeka.

But in many areas of the South, officials used all kinds of tactics to delay desegregation. School districts passed "freedom of choice" policies. These laws allowed students to choose the school they wanted to attend—if there was room. White officials made sure that white schools were filled when blacks applied.

Other school systems required students to pass difficult tests and fill out complex forms before they could move to another school. This made it difficult for blacks to transfer to white schools. If they failed the tests, black students faced more red tape and court trials.

Violent demonstrations prevented other black students from entering white schools. Dorothy Counts, the first black girl to go to a white school in Charlotte, North Carolina, described her ordeal: "I started walking toward the school, a lot of people were just pushing and shoving and calling me names and throwing things, spitting on me and saying . . . 'Nigger go back to Africa'."

Two years after the Supreme Court edict, not one black student had been enrolled in a white school in Alabama, Florida, Georgia, Louisiana, Mississippi, the Carolinas, or Virginia.

A Gallup poll taken in the early 1950s showed that a strong majority of Americans in the East, Midwest, and West favored desegregation. Only one in five Southerners supported the concept. For many in the South, the Warren decisions were red flags waved in front of their faces. It soon became clear that the South would not comply with the ruling without a fight.

In November 1955, James J. Kilpatrick, editor of the Richmond, Virginia, *News Leader*, issued a challenge to Southern white leaders. He urged them to resist desegregation based on the right of "interposition." He claimed that states had a right to reject federal mandates they believed to be unconstitutional. Virginia's legislature approved the interposition doctrine the following February and urged other states to do the same. The vote was overwhelmingly in favor of the resolution.

By early 1956, congressmen from Southern states had joined forces to oppose school desegregation. In March, nineteen senators and seventy-seven House members signed "The Southern Manifesto." The document charged that the Supreme Court's decision was "a clear abuse of judicial power." Forced desegregation of the schools, according to the manifesto, would be "certain to destroy the system of public education in some of the States." The ruling, it continued, created an "explosive and dangerous condition." The document was signed by Senators Strom Thurmond and J. William Fulbright, among others.

Although the signers pledged to "use all lawful

means" to reverse the decision, their action helped spur a massive resistance movement. The Ku Klux Klan, lynch mobs, and violent protesters terrorized Southern blacks and their supporters.

LITTLE ROCK warriors

In 1957, the nation witnessed the first major test of court-ordered school desegregation. The battle at Central High School in Little Rock, Arkansas, became a turning point in the effort to desegregate schools.

Racial tensions had been simmering in Arkansas for some time. After the 1954 *Brown* ruling, several school boards had voted to desegregate, only to face outcries from state officials and local whites. The state's commissioner of education issued a warning to the fourteen school districts with plans to desegregate. He told them that desegregation was against the law in Arkansas, and that local school boards should obey the state law "in the absence of any decree from the U.S. court."

In May 1955, Little Rock's school board submitted plans to desegregate the city's schools. Under the plan, the first black students would attend a white high school in 1957. All grades would be desegregated by 1963.

Orval E. Faubus had unseated Cherry in the primary and won election as governor of Arkansas in 1954. During his bid for reelection in 1956, Faubus pledged that "no school district will be forced to mix the races as long as I am governor of Arkansas." He won the race for governor with 80 percent of the vote. On election day, Arkansas voters approved measures that allowed school boards to reassign students to keep schools segregated. They also voted against "racial mixing" in schools and for a state constitutional amendment to void the Supreme Court's *Brown* ruling.

Tensions increased as the 1957 school term neared. A

cross was burned outside the home of the NAACP's local president, Daisy Bates. A group called the Mothers' League of Little Rock Central High School petitioned Faubus to stop desegregation at the school.

The white mothers who formed the Mothers' League in August 1957 told reporters that their greatest fear was the mixing of the races. This fear—that black boys would date and eventually marry their white daughters—lay at the root of many Americans' opposition to desegregation. Even President Dwight D. Eisenhower expressed sympathy for such views. Following the Supreme Court's ruling in *Brown*, Eisenhower told Chief Justice Earl Warren that Southern segregationists were not "bad people," adding, "All they are concerned about is to see that their sweet little girls are not required to sit in school alongside some big overgrown Negroes."

At the time, state law in Arkansas as well as in other states made it illegal for blacks and whites to marry. Whites supporting such laws viewed them as a way to safeguard the "purity" of the white race. They wanted to make certain that their grandchildren were white and not of mixed race. This, in their view, would ensure white superiority and was a way of holding onto power over blacks.

The mothers also feared violence at the school. Segregationists helped fan these fears by spreading rumors that "Negro gangs were forming" to push desegregation at Central High. Governor Faubus added to the fears by reporting that "revolvers . . . had been taken from students white and black." Even though no evidence backed these claims, some white parents acted on their fears by becoming involved in protests against desegregation.

Others opposed desegregation because they believed the federal government had no right to interfere with the states' decisions, particularly regarding the states' education of their young. To Southerners

ORVAL FAUBUS OF LITTLE ROCK, ARKANSAS, WON HIS GUBERNATORIAL REELEC-
TION CAMPAIGN BY PLEDGING THAT THE SCHOOLS WOULD NOT BE FORCED TO
INTEGRATE UNDER HIS RULE. IN ORDER TO PREVENT DESEGREGATION, HE
ORDERED THE ARKANSAS NATIONAL GUARD TO SURROUND CENTRAL HIGH
SCHOOL SO THAT BLACK STUDENTS COULD NOT ENTER.

who still viewed the Civil War as the "war of Northern
aggression," the order to desegregate schools seemed
like another attempt by the federal government to subjugate the South. They used the states' rights banner to
rally support for segregation.

In late August 1957, the women of the Mothers'
League called Little Rock families to organize a protest
at the high school on opening day. Also participating in
the protest effort were members of the Capital Citizens
Council, the segregationist group formed in the wake of
the Court's first *Brown* verdict.

Many believed they were fighting for their children
and the white race. For example, a Canadian reporter
said Margaret Jackson, a member of the Mothers'
League, "was genuinely convinced that supremacy of
white[s] over the blacks is God given . . . [and] that

allowing Negroes into White schools would promote wide scale miscegenation [race-mixing]." Another Mothers' League member said she feared "inter-racial marriage and the resulting diseases which might arise."

On September 4, 1957, a mob gathered in front of Central High to protest the desegregation plan. Members of the Arkansas National Guard, on orders from Governor Faubus, formed a barricade around the school. During a televised speech the night before, Faubus had said white supremacists from around the state were planning a rally at Central. Faubus had warned blacks to stay away from the school. If the nine students tried to enter Central High, he said, "blood would run in the streets."

NAACP's Bates had called eight of the nine black students and told them to enter the school as a group. One of the students, Elizabeth Eckford, had no telephone and did not get the message. She went to the school alone and was quickly surrounded by the crowd. Children who came to the protest reflected the fears and prejudices of their parents. Hazel Bryan, fifteen and a student at Central High School, was one of many students who participated in the protest with their parents. Hazel watched as the National Guard blocked Elizabeth's way when she tried to enter the school. A photographer captured Hazel's jeering, angry face as she screamed at Elizabeth. The photograph, published in newspapers worldwide, came to symbolize the hatred and unrest swirling around attempts to desegregate schools in the American South. Confused and frightened, Elizabeth stood trapped between the guardsmen and the threatening crowd. A sympathetic white woman and a white *New York Times* reporter escorted Elizabeth onto a bus, and she escaped unharmed.

The National Guard also prevented the remaining eight students from entering the school. The NAACP announced that the students—who became known as the Little Rock Nine—would not attempt to enter the school again until after a court hearing on the matter.

On September 20, a federal judge ruled that Faubus had illegally used the National Guard to prevent desegregation. The governor ordered the troops to leave the school. On September 23, the nine black students tried again to attend Central High. They slipped into the school through a back entrance as an angry mob screamed outside. Tensions mounted as the mob continued its protests. Local police, many of whom sympathized with the white mob, did little to protect the black students. Fearing for the students' safety, officials led them out of the school, again through a side door.

The mob's action forced President Eisenhower's hand. Eisenhower was not enthusiastic about school desegregation and had not taken a strong stand on the issue. But, he told the nation, he could not allow "disorderly mobs" led by "demagogic extremists" to stop school desegregation. "Mob rule," he said, "cannot be allowed to override the decisions of our courts."

Eisenhower ordered the 101st Airborne Division to the school to enforce desegregation and protect the black teenagers. The next day, September 25, one thousand rifle-toting soldiers surrounded the school. Soldiers drove black students to school and walked with them to class. Eisenhower's action showed Americans that the Constitution, the president, and the federal government protected both black and white. Even with soldiers on guard, though, white students unleashed their hostilities. They spat on their black classmates, threw ink and urine on their clothes, forced them into scalding showers, and threatened them and their families.

Recalling that time forty years later, Melba Pattillo Beals told reporters, "I got up every morning, polished

IN RESPONSE TO RIOTING MOBS, PRESIDENT DWIGHT D. EISENHOWER
SENT IN THE 101ST AIRBORNE DIVISION TO ESCORT THE BLACK STUDENTS
INTO THE PREVIOUSLY ALL-WHITE LITTLE ROCK CENTRAL HIGH SCHOOL.

my saddle shoes, and went off to war. It was like being a
soldier on a battlefield."

Hazel Bryan (now Massery) also spoke to reporters
about her role in the events of that period. "I was confused
then," she said. "Now I feel relieved and joyful." Six years
after the mob scene, Massery apologized to Eckford for her
actions. The two women became friends and now talk with
school groups and others about desegregation and their
efforts to promote racial harmony and understanding.

Eight of the nine students finished the year at Central High, and Ernest Green became the first black student to graduate from the school in May 1958. But the battle wasn't over. The Supreme Court in September 1958 ordered Central High to continue desegregation. Instead, Faubus closed the city's four high schools, and citizens voted not to reopen them if black students were enrolled. Classes didn't resume until August 1959. Protests continued, but two of the four high schools did admit several black students. Local police kept the mob at bay.

A year after Little Rock finally reopened, a six-year-old girl named Ruby Bridges became the first black child to desegregate an elementary school under court order. Federal marshals accompanied her on November 14, 1960, to the William Frantz Elementary School in New Orleans. White students boycotted the school, and all but one white teacher refused to teach her. For the first part of the school year, she was the only student at the school. Eventually, some white students returned, but no one played with the little black girl in their midst. The following year, however, whites and blacks attended the school together.

A CALL TO ACTION

Just as the *Brown* decisions and school desegregation inflamed segregationists, the events in Little Rock and New Orleans served as a call to action for black citizens and their white supporters. Like nothing before, the battle at Central High School brought the civil rights struggle home to the entire nation. Historian Doris Kearns Goodwin recalls, as an eleven-year-old, yelling at the television screen as she watched black students being attacked as they tried to enter the white high school. "It was that first activism that led to changing the whole way we looked at America, that led to our being involved with the civil rights movement . . . believing that public action and a few brave kids could change the face of America."

RUBY BRIDGES: BRAVE WALK INTO HISTORY

Six-year-old Ruby Bridges thought it must be Mardi Gras. As she walked to her new school with her mother and four armed federal marshals, angry white people all around them shouted and shook fists in the air. But the little girl, intent on going to school, didn't notice the anger. She just thought people were celebrating and that she was part of a parade.

In a way, Ruby's first day of first grade at William Frantz Public School *was* a celebration. Ruby's march to school marked the first time schools desegregated in Louisiana and four other Southern states. Under court order as a result of the Supreme Court's *Brown* rulings in 1954 and 1955, the Southern states had resisted opening white schools to black students. On November 14, 1960, four young black students—chosen because of their high test scores—entered white schools in New Orleans for the first time. Three of the students went to McDonough school, across town. Ruby was the only one assigned to William Frantz.

When the National Association for the Advancement of Colored People told Ruby's parents that she had been chosen to be among the first to integrate schools in the city, her parents reacted with mixed feelings. Ruby's mother, Lucille, wanted her daughter to go to William Frantz. She thought Ruby would get a better education there, and she believed desegregation would help advance all black children. Ruby's father, Abon, feared for his daughter's safety and was concerned that her attendance at the white school would put the entire family in danger.

As it turned out, the beliefs of both Ruby's parents proved true.

1065801035

On that first day, federal marshals drove Ruby and her mother to school. Two marshals walked in front of them and two behind as they climbed the stairs and entered William Frantz School. While segregationists screamed outside, Ruby and her mother sat in the principal's office. They stayed there all day, watching through the window as angry white parents took their children out of class and away from the school.

The next day, Ruby and her mother and the marshals made the same journey. Outside the school Ruby saw the crowd hoist a small coffin in the air. It held a small black doll. That scared Ruby, but she continued on toward the school.

When she entered the first-grade classroom, Ruby thought she must be early because no one was there. But no other students came to class that day or any other day. For the entire school year, Ruby and her teacher went over the lessons alone. After several months, a few white children began attending other classes in the school. But they all avoided Ruby. One boy told her his mother had said not to play with her "because you're a nigger." It was then that she finally understood that the protests were because of the color of her skin.

Each day Ruby walked with the marshals to her classroom. Ruby never cried and never whimpered. One of the ways she coped was to pray for the people who hurled insults at her. In New Orleans and beyond, protests against desegregation continued. Segregationists rioted throughout the city. Ruby's father was fired from his job because of his daughter's presence at the school. Her grandparents were forced to leave the land in Mississippi they had farmed as sharecroppers for twenty-five years.

Friends, neighbors, and strangers supported Ruby and her family. A neighbor gave her father a job, and others walked behind Ruby on her way to school. Friends kept watch over the family's house; supporters from across the country sent money and letters of encouragement.

Two people, in particular, helped Ruby through the ordeal. Barbara Henry, Ruby's teacher, made school fun despite the turmoil. Ruby never missed a day of school that year. Neither did Henry. Ruby learned about desegregation from her teacher, a New Englander who had taken the job knowing that the school would be desegregated that year. The two of them studied together, ate together, and spent recess inside the classroom playing games and exercising to music. Ruby even adopted a Boston accent from Henry, the first white teacher the little girl had ever known.

The other person in Ruby's struggle was Robert Coles, a child psychiatrist who volunteered to help the young student deal with the situation. He met with her at home each week, and together they talked about all that was happening. Coles later wrote a children's book, *The Story of Ruby Bridges*, about Ruby and her bravery. Ruby's courage also inspired artist Norman Rockwell to paint "The Problem We All Live With," a picture of a small black girl in a sparkling white dress walking determinedly to school with federal marshals on either side and a racial slur defacing the wall.

The months passed. By June only a few protesters waited outside the school. The next September, Ruby returned to William Frantz School as a second-grader. This time other students joined her—both black and white. Desegregation—thanks to Ruby and other brave students like her—had finally been achieved in New Orleans.

After graduating from a desegregated high school,

Ruby Bridges went to business school and worked as a travel agent. She married and had four children. After Coles's book was published, Ruby Bridges (now Hall) began speaking to school groups about desegregation and her role in it. She also reunited with Henry. Today, the two women often tell their story together. Through the Ruby Bridges Foundation, they speak to school children about racism and the resegregation of schools. William Frantz School, for example, has mostly black students because white families have moved from the area.

"We as adults have to create the environment that brings these kids together," Ruby Bridges Hall told a reporter in 2000. "The best ammunition we can give kids is to tell them they are in a unique position. They can do something that we as adults haven't been seen to get past yet. They can change the world."

Even before Little Rock, however, activists had begun to fight segregation in other areas of Southern life. On December 1, 1955, Rosa Parks, a black woman who worked as a seamstress, refused to go to the back of the bus in Montgomery, Alabama. Her act led to a successful bus boycott, headed by the Reverend Martin Luther King Jr., a Montgomery minister. The Supreme Court in 1956 banned segregation on public transportation. The ruling, in *Gayle* v. *Browder*, overturned *Plessy* once and for all.

The success of the bus boycott inspired other protests. Black teenagers held sit-ins at lunch counters reserved for whites. "Freedom riders"—blacks and whites who rode together on buses, trains, and planes— tested segregation laws throughout the South. By 1956, Baltimore had opened its beaches to blacks, Atlanta's golf courses allowed black players, and Michigan and Missouri had banned segregation in public housing. The following year, Congress passed the first civil rights bill since Reconstruction to protect the voting rights of Southern blacks. The law, however, had little effect. Local juries decided cases involving violations of the law. Since jurors had to be registered voters and few blacks were allowed to register, violators rarely faced punishment.

Over the next dozen years, the Warren Court and new federal laws lifted many of the barriers facing blacks. The Court struck down segregation in parks, restaurants, hotels, libraries, and courtrooms. The race of candidates could no longer be listed on ballots. The Court invalidated laws banning marriage between blacks and whites.

Landmark CIVIL RIGHTS ACT

Activism reached a fever pitch in the 1960s. Protesters, both black and white, joined Martin Luther King Jr. in nonviolent marches in Birmingham, Alabama. Television news cameras captured local police attacking the pro-testers and blasting them with fire hoses. The outrage that followed helped President John F. Kennedy win support for a civil rights proposal that would form the basis of the Civil Rights Act of 1964.

Kennedy was slow to take action in the civil rights efforts at first, resisting King's pleas for federal help to quell violence aimed at protesters. By 1962, however, the president had joined the fight for civil rights reforms, beginning with a voter education project designed to increase the number of black voters. Later that year, Kennedy sent federal troops to Mississippi to protect James Meredith, the first black student to enroll at the state university. In June 1963, President Kennedy urged Americans to end racial discrimination and announced his intention to ask Congress to pass a law to desegregate public facilities.

The president recognized that segregation was not just a Southern problem. The North had its share of segregated schools. Inner-city schools had mostly black students as whites moved to suburbs or enrolled their children in private schools. In many suburban communities, whites refused to sell homes to blacks. This resulted in "de facto" segregation—racial separation that resulted from circumstances rather than being required by law.

"We must recognize that segregation in education—and I mean de facto segregation in the North as well as the proclaimed segregation in the South—brings with it serious handicaps to a large population," Kennedy said.

After Kennedy's assassination in November 1963, President Lyndon Johnson pushed through the Civil Rights Act of 1964. The landmark legislation banned racial discrimination and instructed the federal government to enforce the law. Over the next decade, the Justice Department sued five hundred school districts for discrimination.

Back to court

Ten years after the first *Brown* ruling, desegregation in schools remained a mix of successes and failures. In states bordering the Deep South, more than 55 percent of black students attended racially mixed schools, but only 1 percent of black children had been allowed into white schools in the Deep South. Mississippi had yet to desegregate one school.

Virginia's Prince Edward County, the site of one of the original school segregation cases, refused to pay for desegregated public schools. County officials closed public schools for five years, from 1959 to 1964. During that time, a private foundation ran an academy in the county for white children only. The county and state provided grants to the white students to help pay their tuition.

Some black students went to stay with relatives in communities where they could attend school. The NAACP and the American Friends Association provided tutors for other black children. Many, however, had no schooling at all. Black leaders and others objected to such unequal treatment. In 1960, the NAACP took the matter to court.

Under pressure, white leaders offered to set up an all-black private school, which would charge students an annual tuition of $240. Black leaders, however, turned down the offer. They continued to push for desegregated schools and did not want to jeopardize their court case. They also did not trust that white school officials would open such a school and doubted that, if it did open, it would be equal to the all-white academy.

In 1963, a nonprofit organization, the Prince Edward Free School Association, opened a free school in the county that accepted both black and white students. Organized with the help of state officials and financed with private donations and grants, the school was set up as a temporary, one-year substitute for public schools. More than 1,500 black children and four white children enrolled in the school in September 1963.

After making its way through lower courts, the NAACP case—*Griffin* v. *School Board*—came before the Supreme Court in 1964. The Court used the opportunity to sharpen its *Brown* rulings. "The time for mere 'deliberate speed' has run out," wrote Justice Black in the majority opinion, "and that phrase can no longer justify denying these Prince Edward County schoolchildren their constitutional rights to an education equal to that afforded by the public schools in other parts of Virginia." No longer would the county be permitted to avoid operating desegregated public schools.

The Court showed it had run out of patience with the South's delays in deciding a 1968 case involving another Virginia school board. The Court ruled in *Green* v. *County School Board of New Kent County* that "freedom of choice" plans could no longer be used to avoid school desegregation. Such systems were illegal, the Court ruled. The justices ordered school boards to desegregate their schools and eliminate discrimination "root and branch."

eight
Darkness and Light

BLACK RIGHTS ADVOCATES made great strides in the 1960s. During those years, Congress passed a strong civil rights act; the Voting Rights Act of 1965 gave many more black citizens the vote; and the Fair Housing Act of 1968 attacked discrimination in private house sales. The Twenty-fourth Amendment, eliminating the requirement that citizens pay a poll tax or other fee before being allowed to vote, was ratified in 1964. The poll tax had been used in the past to prevent black citizens from voting. In addition, the federal government began providing funds to help schools desegregate. Courts ordered school boards to desegregate teachers as well as students.

During that decade, black leaders gained national status. Martin Luther King Jr.'s efforts received worldwide attention, particularly after he received the Nobel Peace Prize in 1964. Edward Brooke, R-Mass., became the first black to serve in the U.S. Senate since Reconstruction. Thurgood Marshall, who had played such a crucial role in the *Brown* cases, was appointed to the U.S. Supreme Court in 1967. The mainstream successes of black entertainers such as Bill Cosby, Sammy Davis Jr., and Sidney Poitier, the first black actor to win

PRESIDENT LYNDON JOHNSON NOT ONLY SIGNED THE CIVIL RIGHTS ACT INTO
LAW IN 1964, BUT, IN 1967, HE APPOINTED THE FIRST AFRICAN AMERICAN TO THE
SUPREME COURT: THURGOOD MARSHALL (RIGHT), WHO HAD SUCCESSFULLY
ARGUED *BROWN* V. *BOARD OF EDUCATION.*

an Academy Award for Best Actor, demonstrated the
progress blacks had made in American popular culture.

Even with these gains, school desegregation continued to make slow progress. A lower court's ruling in a
1969 suit allowed thirty-three Mississippi school districts
to delay desegregation once again. In deciding the case,
Alexander v. *Holmes County Board of Education*, the
Supreme Court later that year issued a stern, no-nonsense
order to end segregation immediately. Using "all deliberate speed" for desegregation, wrote Chief Justice Burger,
"is no longer constitutionally permissible."

Responding to the ruling, Robert Finch, secretary of the
Department of Health, Education, and Welfare, ordered
Mississippi to desegregate its schools. When President
Richard M. Nixon delayed the order, Finch and other top
officials resigned in protest. Catering to Southern white

leaders, Nixon had done little to help the desegregation effort. Despite his actions, federal judges enforced the Supreme Court's ruling. This time, Southern schools complied. In the fifteen years since the *Brown* ruling, people finally had accepted desegregation as inevitable.

Tackling De Facto Segregation

Attention now turned to the de facto segregation John F. Kennedy had mentioned. This racial separation by neighborhood could be found in the North as well as the South. The Court in *Brown* v. *Board of Education* had ruled that states could no longer operate separate schools for blacks and whites. These new cases, however, went beyond desegregation. Their goal was to integrate schools. In addition to opening schools to students of all races, school systems would be required to ensure that their schools were racially mixed in percentages that mirrored the ethnic background of their citizens. To accomplish that goal, courts began ordering students from one area to be bused to other areas. The first such case to reach the Supreme Court, *Swann* v. *Charlotte-Mecklenburg Board of Education*, concerned six-year-old James Swann's court claim that the schools in Charlotte, North Carolina, were not desegregated. Dr. John A. Finger, an expert appointed by the lower court, devised a plan to bus students across district lines to achieve integration. The plan, however, met with violent opposition from white parents and others, including President Nixon.

In 1971, the Supreme Court issued a unanimous decision in the *Swann* case to allow busing if that was what it took to integrate schools. Written by Chief Justice Warren Burger, the decision acknowledged that neighborhood schools were preferred, all things being equal. "But all things are not equal in a system that has been deliberately

RESISTANCE TO INTEGRATION WAS OFTEN AS STRONG IN THE NORTH AS IN THE SOUTH. CONGRESSWOMAN LOUISE DAY HICKS (RIGHT) OF BOSTON WAS NOTORIOUS AS A LEADER IN THE FIGHT AGAINST COURT-ORDERED BUSING.

constructed and maintained to enforce racial segregation," Burger noted. The solution, he added, might be "administratively awkward, inconvenient, and even bizarre in some situations and may impose burdens on some." Even so, Burger said, such measures were unavoidable in the effort "to eliminate the dual school systems." The Court viewed solutions such as busing as temporary. It ruled Charlotte would have to obey the lower court's order to integrate the city's schools by busing students.

Few liked busing as a solution. Parents and students objected to long bus rides to schools outside their neighborhoods. People wanted control over where their children attended school. In some areas protests became violent. After the ruling, terrorists in Pontiac,

Michigan, exploded ten buses and thousands marched in a mock funeral to protest forced busing. Television cameras captured mobs of angry parents shouting at scared black children. Once again, racial unrest swirled around the schools as a shocked nation watched.

In March 1972 President Nixon asked Congress to delay busing, and Congress considered a bill to amend the Constitution to ban it. Both measures failed, but it showed the widespread opposition to the measure. Even many supporters of integration disapproved of busing. According to polls at the time, more than 75 percent of Americans favored school integration. An equal number opposed busing as a way to achieve it.

courts step in

While the South gradually integrated schools, the North and West lagged behind. In 1973 only 28 percent of the black students in those areas attended integrated schools. Meanwhile, 46 percent of Southern blacks went to schools with white classmates. As the campaign to integrate schools moved north, the busing controversy focused on Boston. Black parents filed a class action suit to force Boston schools to integrate. In 1974 U.S. District Judge W. Arthur Garrity Jr. ordered Boston to bus black students to white schools and vice versa. In his ruling, the judge said, the Boston School Committee "had knowingly carried out a systematic program of segregation affecting all of the city's students, teachers, and school facilities and [had] intentionally brought about and maintained a dual school system."

Garrity soon became known as "the most hated man in Boston." On the first day of class, September 12, 1974, students staged a massive boycott. On the second day and for many days afterward, violent actions by unruly mobs led the governor to put the National Guard on alert status.

yonkers: two decades of court battles

The city of Yonkers, New York, struggled with de facto segregation for more than twenty years. In 1980 whites lived in the eastern section of the city, while blacks and Hispanics lived in the southwestern part. As a result, the schools in each section had few students of other races. The federal government sued to force the city to integrate both its housing and its schools. In 1981, the National Association for the Advancement of Colored People (NAACP) joined the suit.

The district court decided that the city had intentionally kept black students out of white schools and black residents from settling in white neighborhoods. To remedy the situation, the court in 1986 ordered Yonkers to adopt several measures to integrate its schools.

These measures included:

- Setting up special courses—called magnet programs— to attract white students to minority schools.

- Allowing students a choice of school to attend. Under the "controlled choice" system, the choices were honored if they furthered integration.

- Busing children to schools outside their neighborhoods.

The court appointed a federal monitor to oversee the campaign. The schools were to be integrated by the 1987–1988 school year.

In September 1987, the court agreed to add the state of New York to the court action. This was done to force the state to help pay for the cost of the desegregation programs.

Throughout the process, the city battled the integration order in court. Opponents charged that the campaign forced white residents and businesses to move out of the city. Even some black citizens eventually protested that the city should be allowed to run the schools once gains had been made. According to some experts, the effort to integrate the schools cost the city and state $500 million.

Twenty-two years after the original suit, the city's schools were more diverse than they were in 1980. But black and Hispanic students continued to score lower than white students in English and math. In March 2002 the various sides in the dispute agreed to a settlement that would end federal supervision of the city's schools. Under the plan, approved by the court, the state agreed to pay $300 million over five years to improve education programs for black and Hispanic students.

The agreement did not solve all of Yonkers' school problems. In 2003, minority students had made gains in test scores, but they still lagged behind white students. A year after the court settlement, the city had yet to hire a settlement compliance officer. And even with the state funds, the city's school board had a $4.2 million budget gap.

After living under court orders for so long, though, school officials and residents were happy to see an end to federal monitoring. "It's like having someone camped out in your backyard who every time you step outside, looks to see what you're doing and how you're doing it," said Marvin J. Feldberg, principal of School 22 in Yonkers.

But he agreed that the lawsuits did help the city deal with segregation. NAACP leaders noted that the court orders also brought needed money and many improvements to the schools that would not have happened otherwise. These benefited all the city's students, they said.

Feldberg's school is a good example of the changes made since the integration efforts first began. The elementary school, whose students once were almost all white, now is called the "Multicultural Academy." It attracts both black and white students from all over the city.

The most violent encounters occurred at South Boston High School, in the mostly white Irish section of the city. Police had to escort black students into school and patrol hallways. Racial fights broke out almost daily. Groups of white mothers, angry at having no say over where their children attended school, challenged police.

Other cities in the West and the North began similar busing programs, often under protest. San Francisco, for example, spent more than $200 million on a busing system ordered by the court in 1982.

For the next fifteen years, the federal court oversaw desegregation in Boston schools. During that time, the court issued some four hundred orders relating to the city's schools. Gradually racial tension lessened. But many blamed busing for the large numbers of white families moving from urban areas to the suburbs. This "white flight" increased the percentage of blacks and Hispanics in the cities and made it even more difficult to achieve integration.

A Supreme Court ruling in 1974 set back the efforts to fight segregation caused by white flight. In *Milliken* v. *Bradley*, a split Court ruled that Detroit could not include outlying school districts in its plan to desegregate inner-city schools. Because the outlying areas had not violated desegregation orders, the Court ruled that Detroit's plan was "wholly impermissible." Schools did not have to have "any particular racial balance" in every school or classroom, according to the decision. The ruling also noted that local people should be able to control their schools. The opinion was a major defeat for those trying to integrate inner-city schools.

In the end, busing policies failed. Busing did not lead to higher test scores by black children. Inside the integrated schools, black students clustered together while white students did the same. Some critics argued that busing only increased the hostility between the races. It wasted money, time, and energy, they said, that could have been better spent on education.

In 1989, the federal court withdrew from the Boston school system. For the next ten years officials enrolled students in the school of their choice, provided the balance between black and white students was retained. In 1999, twenty-five years after Judge Garrity's initial order, the Boston School Committee discontinued the choice program after white parents sued to end it. The vote meant that students would be required to attend schools in their own neighborhoods. Supporters cheered the vote. They said the return to neighborhood schools would encourage

DESPITE STRONG RESISTANCE TO THE BUSING OF BLACK CHILDREN TO PREVIOUSLY ALL-WHITE SCHOOLS IN BOSTON AND OTHER PARTS OF MASSACHUSETTS, SOME FIVE THOUSAND PUPILS WERE TRANSFERRED TO NEW SCHOOLS IN SPRINGFIELD'S COURT-ORDERED BUSING PLAN ON SEPTEMBER 16, 1974.

parents to become more involved in their children's education. Others feared, however, that the new system would mean a return to de facto segregation.

Beginning in the early 1990s, the Supreme Court under conservative Chief Justice William H. Rehnquist began instructing lower courts to withdraw as supervisors of school integration programs. In a 1991 decision, in *Board of Education of Oklahoma City* v. *Dowell*, the Court ruled that "ultimately, control over schools must be returned to local school districts." In the same case, the Court ruled that school systems needed only to demonstrate that they were complying in good faith with previous court-ordered desegregation and had eliminated traces of former segregation "to the extent practicable."

In another case, *Freeman* v. *Pitts*, decided in 1992, the Court went further in lifting court-ordered integration programs from schools. Under the ruling, the Court would no longer require schools to have racial percentages in balance with the local community. "Racial balance is not to be achieved for its own sake," wrote Justice Anthony Kennedy in the majority opinion. He also noted that resegregation—the return to schools attended by children of only one race—was not unconstitutional if it was "a product not of state action but of private choices." In other words, resegregation might be tolerated if it was the result of housing patterns, but not if the local community voted to segregate schools.

With these rulings, the Court expressed willingness to turn over responsibility for integration to local school officials and gave a nod of acceptance to de facto segregation.

AFFIRMATIVE ACTION

While public schools struggled to integrate, colleges faced their own difficulties in offering equal opportunities to minority students. Since the 1964 Civil Rights Act, the federal government had required employers not to discriminate against blacks and other minorities when hiring and promoting. In 1965, Lyndon Johnson issued an executive order to federal contractors to "take affirmative action" to ensure that members of minorities were given a fair number of jobs. Congress and government agencies later expanded Johnson's order to other areas. These affirmative action programs, as they were called, sought to help members of minorities who had been discriminated against. Those who supported the programs argued that giving certain advantages to minorities was the only way to overcome the lack of opportunities these groups had suffered in the past.

As part of this effort, the Department of Health, Education, and Welfare funded programs set up by colleges and universities to increase the number of minority students and faculty members. Like many colleges, the medical school of the University of California at Davis offered a special admissions program for disadvantaged applicants. Under the program, 16 percent of those enrolled in the school had to be minority students.

In 1974, Allan Bakke sued the school for illegally denying him admission. Bakke, a white man, had higher grades and better test scores than some of the black students enrolled under the school's special admissions program. This "reverse discrimination," Bakke charged, denied him equal treatment under the law solely because he was white.

The Supreme Court agreed, at least in part. In a 1978 split decision, the Court ordered the school to admit Bakke and struck down the use of quotas in affirmative action programs. But the Court allowed such programs to consider race as one factor in choosing students. Justice Lewis F. Powell Jr. voted with four other justices in ordering

Bakke's admittance. But Powell, in a separate opinion, argued that there was a "compelling state interest" in racial diversity among students. The decision left colleges to ponder exactly how they should implement their programs.

The situation became more confusing when the Court refused to overturn a 1996 decision of the Fifth Circuit Court of Texas on affirmative action programs. In that case, *Texas* v. *Hopwood*, the lower court ruled that the University of Texas Law School should not consider race when admitting students. The school had considered race in order to have a diverse student body and to remedy past discrimination against minority students. Neither goal, the lower court ruled, was compelling enough to allow the school to give minority students preferential treatment.

On June 23, 2003, the Supreme Court ruled on two other affirmative action cases, *Grutter* v. *Bollinger* (University of Michigan Law School) and *Gratz* v. *Bollinger* (University of Michigan). Again issuing a split decision, the Court by one vote allowed the University of Michigan's Law School to continue its affirmative action program. At the same time, however, the Court struck down the program used to select undergraduates at the school. The difference between the two proved crucial.

The plan supported by the Court required college officials to look at each applicant and consider all factors, including race. Instead of the individual approach, the undergraduate program used a point system that included race. Because the undergraduate program used race in a "mechanical way," it could not be allowed, according to the decision. President George W. Bush had asked the Court to ban both policies.

In the decision she wrote for the majority in the *Grutter* case, Justice Sandra Day O'Connor strongly supported admitting students of all races as a way of creating a more equal society. "Effective participation by members of all racial and ethnic groups in the civil life of our nation is essential if the dream of one nation, indivisible, is to be realized," Justice O'Connor wrote. She added the hope that affirmative action programs would achieve the goal of a more equal society and should "no longer be necessary" in twenty-five years.

The two rulings gave colleges better guidelines for affirmative action programs.

MIXED REVIEWS

Almost fifty years after the *Brown* ruling, its goal of desegregating the schools receives mixed reviews. Results from a 2003 study by the Civil Rights Project at Harvard suggest that schools are becoming more segregated. In many cases, this has occurred because white families have moved away from the cities, where a majority of blacks and Hispanics live. In addition, many of the court-supervised integration plans have ended, and recent rulings have been less supportive of court-ordered integration.

According to the Harvard study, "A Multiracial Society with Segregated Schools: Are We Losing the Dream?," black children in the Northeast and the Midwest are the most likely to be concentrated in inner cities. One-fourth of the black children in these areas attend poor, inner-city schools that have very few whites. Students in Seattle and other Northwest cities, however, live in more integrated neighborhoods, and their schools are more mixed. Schools in the South remain the most integrated.

The trend toward resegregation has also hit suburban areas. Since the mid-1980s, schools in suburbia, especially in the South, have become less and less integrated.

The study, based on the U.S. census of 2000, found that the number of black students attending schools with a majority of white students has dipped to 1968 levels. In addition, black students still lag behind white students in school achievement tests.

The Harvard study also notes that the number of minority students in the nation has steadily grown. Some 40 percent of all public school students are now nonwhite. This is almost double the percentage of minority students during the 1960s.

There is progress. Blacks and whites live, work, and play together all over America. Although racial tension still exists, angry mobs no longer block a black student's entrance to school. Black leaders and celebrities such as Secretary of State Colin Powell and National Security Adviser Condoleezza Rice, basketball legend Michael Jordan, and television talk show host Oprah Winfrey are widely admired by Americans of all races. Ten times as many black students now attend college as in the 1950s. And a black student is just as likely as a white student to graduate from high school.

Certainly, *Brown* v. *Board of Education* played a major role in that progress. "The country would have been segregated for a long, long time had the Warren Court not ruled segregation in schools unconstitutional," says historian Roger Wilkins.

Zelma Henderson, one of the original plaintiffs in the *Brown* case, agrees: "When you get right down to it, the message of the *Brown* decision . . . is really that all human beings of all races are created equal," she says. "We went to the Supreme Court of the United States to affirm that fact, and we won."

TIMELINE

1950	*Briggs* v. *Elliott* filed in U.S. District Court
1951	*Bolling* v. *Sharpe* heard in U.S. District Court
February 1951	*Oliver Brown* v. *Board of Education of Topeka* filed in U.S. District Court for the District of Kansas
May 1951	*Briggs* v. *Elliott* argued in U.S. District Court
May 1951	*Davis* v. *County School Board of Prince Edward County* filed in U.S. District Court in Richmond
June 1951	District court rules against *Briggs*
June 1951	District court hears *Brown* case
July 1951	*Briggs* case appealed to U.S. Supreme Court
August 1951	District court rules against *Brown*
September 1951	*Brown* case appealed to U.S. Supreme Court
October 1951	*Belton* v. *Gebhart* and *Bulah* v. *Gebhart* go to trial in Delaware Chancery Court
February 1952	District court hears *Davis* case
March 1952	District court rules in favor of school board in *Davis* case; Davis appeals to Supreme Court
April 1952	Delaware Chancery Court rules in favor of *Belton* and *Bulah*; orders white schools to desegregate
August 28, 1952	Delaware Supreme Court upholds Chancery Court ruling on *Bulah* and *Belton*; state appeals to Supreme Court
October 1952	Supreme Court joins *Brown*, *Briggs*, *Davis*, *Belton*, and *Bulah* cases and announces it will hear *Bolling* at same time
December 9–11, 1952	Supreme Court hears arguments in joined cases and *Bolling*
June 1953	Supreme Court schedules rearguments for October
September 1953	Supreme Court Chief Justice Frederick Vinson dies; Earl Warren nominated to fill post as Chief Justice
December 7–9, 1953	*Brown et al.* reargued before Supreme Court
May 17, 1954	Supreme Court issues decisions in *Brown*, *Bolling*
October 1954	Justice Robert Jackson dies; John Marshall Harlan nominated to fill post
April 11–14, 1955	Brown cases reargued on how to integrate (*Brown II*)
May 31, 1955	Supreme Court issues decision in *Brown II*
September 4, 1957	First day of school for "Little Rock Nine" in Arkansas
November 14, 1960	First day of school for Ruby Bridges in New Orleans

notes

Chapter 1

p. 11, par. 2, Marjorie G. Fribourg. *The Supreme Court in American History: Ten Great Decisions—The People, the Times and the Issues.* Philadelphia: Macrae Smith Company, 1965.

p. 15, par. 3, Brown Foundation for Educational Equity, Excellence and Research. *"Brown* v. *Board of Education* Orientation Handbook, Combined Brown Cases, 1951–1954, *Briggs* v. *Elliot"* http://brownvboard.org/research/handbook/combined/briggs. htm (Accessed Sept. 3, 2003.)

p. 16, par. 3, Richard Kluger. *Simple Justice.* New York: Alfred A. Knopf, 1976.

p. 17, par. 2, Ibid.

Chapter 2

p. 20, par. 2, Fourteenth Amendment.

p. 22, par. 1, Richard Kluger. *Simple Justice.* New York: Alfred A. Knopf, 1976.

p. 23, par. 3, *United States* v. *State of Louisiana*, 25 F. Supp. 353; 1963 U.S. Dist. LEXIS 10307, Nov. 27, 1963. http://www.law. stetson.edu/courses/casedigests/usvla.pdf (Accessed May 11, 2004.)

p. 24, par. 1, *The Slaughterhouse Cases*, 83 US 36 (1873).

p. 24, par. 3, Justice Stephen Field dissent, *The Slaughterhouse Cases*, 83 US 36 (1873).

p. 25, par. 3, Civil Rights Act of 1875.

p. 25, par. 4–p. 27, par. 2, *Plessy* v. *Ferguson*, 163 US 537 (1896).

p. 27, par. 3–p. 28, par. 1, Ibid.

p. 28, par. 2 , "Ties that Bind: The Great Migration," The Mattatuck Historical Society. http://mattatuckmuseum.org/ties/two/two.htm (Accessed May 11, 2004.)

p. 30, par. 1, Kentucky brief and arguments, *Berea College* v. *Commonwealth of Kentucky*, 94 S.W. 623 (1906).

p. 30, par. 3, "African American Odyssey," "American Memory," Historical Collections for the National Digital Library, Library of

Congress. http://memory.loc.gov/ammem/aaohtml/exhibit/aopart7.html
(Accessed Sept. 10, 2003.)

p. 31, par. 1, "CCC, Civilian Conservation Corps," Farm Security Administration.
http://www.livinghistoryfarm.org/farminginthe30s/water_12.html
(Accessed May 11, 2004.)

p. 31, par. 2, Executive Order 8802.

Chapter 3

pp. 33–37, Douglas O. Linder. *Before Brown: Charles H. Houston and the Gaines, 2000.* http://www.law.umkc.edu/faculty/projects/ftrials/conlaw/houstonessay.html (Accessed May 12, 2004.)

p. 35, par. 3, *Missouri Ex Rel. Gaines v. Canada, Registrar of the University of Missouri, et al.,* 305 U.S. 337 (1938).

p. 35, par. 4–6, *The New York Times,* Dec. 13, 1938, pp. 1, 2.

p. 37, par. 6, "MU Names Black Culture Center, Honors Gaines, O'Fallon Oldham," University of Missouri press release, Feb. 26, 2002. http://www.missouri.edu/~news/releases/febmar02/bccrenaming2.html (Accessed Jan. 9, 2004.)

p. 39, par. 5, Richard Kluger. *Simple Justice.* New York: Alfred A. Knopf, 1976.

p. 40, par. 3, *Houston Informer,* Jan. 1950. http://www.law.du.edu/russell/lh/sweatt/inf/HI-index.htm (Accessed Sept. 11, 2003.)

p. 41, par. 1, "Arguments before the Court," *The United States Law Week,* Vol. 18, No. 39, p. 3277, April 11, 1950.

p. 41, par. 4–p. 42, par. 6, *Houston Informer,* April 8, 1950. http://www.law.du.edu/russell/lh/sweatt/inf/HI-index.htm (Accessed Sept. 11, 2003.)

p. 43, par. 2–4, *Sweatt v. Painter,* 339 U.S. 629 (1950).

Chapter 4

p. 44, par. 2, Fifth Amendment.

p. 44, par. 2, *Meyer v. Nebraska* 262 U.S. 390 (1923).

p. 46–48 Iowa Court Information System.
http://www.judicial.state.ia.us/students/6 (Accessed Nov. 3, 2003.)
The Supreme Court Historical Society.
http://www.supremecourthistory.org (Accessed Nov. 3, 2003.)
Administrative Office of the U.S. Courts.
http://www.uscourts.gov (Accessed Nov. 3, 2003.)

p. 48, par. 1 (text), Oral Arguments, Thurgood Marshall, *Briggs v. Elliott,* 347 U.S. 497 (1954).

p. 48, par. 2 (text), "Historical Documents and Speeches: *Briggs v. Elliott,*" http://www.historicaldocuments.com/BriggsvElliott.htm (Accessed May 11, 2004.)

p. 49, par. 1, "*Briggs* v. *Elliott* Timeline," *The State,* June 1, 2003. www.thestate.com/mld/thestate/news/special_packages/briggs/5978988.htm (Accessed Sept. 11, 2003.)

p. 50, par. 1, Philip B. Kurland and Gerhard Casper. *Landmark Briefs* and *Arguments of the Supreme Court of the United States: Constitutional Law,* "Brown v. Board of Education (1954 & 1955)," vol. 49. Arlington, VA: University Publications of America Inc., 1975.

p. 50, par. 3–p. 51, par. 1, Richard Kluger. *Simple Justice*. New York: Alfred A. Knopf, 1976.

p. 52, par. 2, Ibid.

p. 52, par. 3, Ibid.

p. 53, par. 1, Ibid.

p. 54, par. 1–2, *Belton v. Gebhart*, Delaware Court of Chancery, 32 Del.Ch. at 359, 87 A.2d at 870, Opinion, 9.

p. 55, par. 3–5, *Davis v. County School Board of Prince Edward County*, Civ. A. No. 1333, U.S. District Court, Eastern District of Virginia, at Richmond, 103 F. Supp. 337.

Chapter 5

p. 57, par. 4, Richard Kluger. *Simple Justice*. New York: Alfred A. Knopf, 1976, p. 540.

p. 58, par. 1, Ibid.

p. 58, par. 2–3, Philip B. Kurland and Gerhard Casper. *Landmark Briefs and Arguments of the Supreme Court of the United States: Constitutional Law,* "Brown v. Board of Education (1954 & 1955)," vol. 49. Arlington, VA.: University Publications of America Inc., 1975.

p. 59, par. 2–p. 65, par. 4, Ibid.

p. 65, par. 7–p. 67, par. 4, Kluger. *Simple Justice*.

p. 67, par. 5–p. 68, par. 1, Associate Justice Tom C. Clark. "Memorandum to Supreme Court Justices." Tom C. Clark Papers, U.S. Supreme Court Case Files. Box A2, Folder 3. Rare Books & Special Collections, Tarlton Law Library, University of Texas at Austin. http://www.law.du.edu/ russell/lh/sweatt/docs/clarkmemo.htm (Accessed Sept. 16, 2003.)

p. 68, par. 2, Kluger. *Simple Justice*.

p. 69, par. 3, Tom Wicker. *Dwight D. Eisenhower*. New York: Times Books/Henry Holt & Company, 2002.

p. 70, par. 1–p. 71, par. 6, Kurland. *Landmark Briefs and Arguments*, vol. 49A.

p. 72, par. 1, 4, 6, Kluger. *Simple Justice*.

p. 75, par. 1, Paul Craig Roberts and Lawrence M. Stratton. *The Brown Decision, The New Color Line: How Quotas and Privileges Destroy Democracy*. Washington, DC: Regnery Publishing, 1997. http://www.lewrockwell.com/orig/brown.html (Accessed May 11, 2004.)

p. 75, par. 3, "Transcriptions of Conversations between Justice William O. Douglas and Professor Walter F. Murphy," Cassette No. 13, Dec. 17, 1962, Princeton University. http://infoshare1.princeton.edu/ libraries/firestone/rbsc/finding_aids/douglas/douglas13.html (Accessed May 12, 2004.)

p. 75, par. 5–p. 76, par. 1, E. Barrett Prettyman Jr. "Thoughts on Justice Jackson's Unpublished Opinion of *Brown* v. *Board of Education*," Oct. 8, 2003. http://www.roberthjackson.org/

Speeches_About_Jackson_BrownvBoard.asp (Accessed May 12, 2004.)

p. 76, par. 2, John B. Fassett. "Mr. Justice Reed and *Brown* v. *The Board of Education,*" *Supreme Court Historical Society 1986 Yearbook*. http://www.supremecourthistory.org/04_library/subs_volumes/04_c18_k.html (Accessed May 11, 2004.)

p. 76, par. 3, D. J. Herda. *Mr. Chief Justice: Earl Warren and the Reticence of America*. http://amsaw.org/swetkyagency/submission synopsis-herda-justiceseries-earlwarren.html (Accessed May 12, 2004.)

p. 77, par. 2, *Brown* v. *Board of Education of Topeka*, 347 U.S. 483 (1954).

p. 77, par. 2, Juan Williams. "Marshall's Law," *Washington Post Magazine*, Jan. 7, 1990. http://www.thurgoodmarshall.com/speeches/tmlaw_ article.htm (Accessed May 12, 2004.)

Chapter 6

p. 78, par. 2– p. 80, par. 3, *Brown* v. *Board of Education of Topeka*, 347 U.S. 483 (1954).
David Pitts. "*Brown* v. *Board of Education*: The Supreme Court Decision That Changed A Nation," *Issues of Democracy*, vol. 4, no. 2, Sept. 1999. http://usinfo.state.gov/journals/itdhr/0999/ijde/pitts.htm (Accessed Sept. 11, 2003.)

p. 81, par. 3, *The New York Times*, May 18, 1954. http://www.landmark cases.org/brown/reaction.html (Accessed Sept. 11, 2003.)

p. 81, par. 4, *Defender* (Chicago), May 18, 1954. http://www.landmark cases.org/brown/reaction.html. (Accessed Sept. 11, 2003.)

p. 82, par. 1–3, "Immediate Reaction to the Decision: Comparing Regional Media Coverage," Landmark Cases: *Brown* v. *Board of Education* (1954), Street Law & the Supreme Court Historial Society. http://www.landmarkcases.org/brown/reaction.html (Accessed May 12, 2004.)

p. 82, par. 4, Richard Kluger. *Simple Justice*. New York: Alfred A. Knopf, 1976.

p. 83, par. 1, "Education and Civil Rights in America 1945 to 1968," The Association of Teachers' Websites. http://www.historylearningsite.co.uk/USAeduc.htm (Accessed Sept. 11, 2003.)

p. 83, par. 2, *Atlanta Constitution*, May 18, 1954. http://books.nap.edu/books/0309083036/html/208.html (Accessed May 12, 2004.)

p. 83, par. 3, Dick Pettys, "Former Georgia Governor Herman Talmadge dies at 88," Associated Press, March 21, 2002.

p. 86, par. 3, Melba Pattillo Beals. *Warriors Don't Cry: A Searing Memoir of the Battle to Integrate Little Rock's Central High*. New York: Washington Square Press, 1995, pp. 22–26.

p. 87, par. 6, Kluger. *Simple Justice*.

p. 88, par. 2–p. 91, par. 1, Philip B. Kurland and Gerhard Casper. *Landmark Briefs and Arguments of the Supreme Court of the United States: Constitutional Law*, "Brown v. Board of Education (1954 & 1955)," vol. 49A. Arlington, VA: University Publications of America Inc., 1975.

p. 91, par. 3, *Brown v. Board of Education of Topeka*, 349 U.S. 294 (1955).

p. 91, par. 4, Kluger. *Simple Justice*.

Chapter 7

p. 92, par. 5–p. 93, par. 1, Bernard Schwartz. *Swann's Way: The School Busing Case and the Supreme Court*. New York: Oxford University Press, 1986.

p. 93, par. 3, "The Gallup Poll: 65 Years of Polling History–Timeline Of Polling History: Events That Shaped the United States, and the World," Gallup Organization. http://www.gallup.com/poll/focus/ polls_this_century_events.asp (Accessed Oct. 6, 2003.)

p. 93, par. 5–p. 94, The Southern Manifesto.

p. 94, par. 3, "Time-Line: The Stage Is Set." Little Rock Newspapers Inc. http://www.ardemgaz.com/prev/central/CHSmain.html (Accessed May 12, 2004.)

p. 95, par. 2, Earl Warren, *The Memories of Earl Warren*. New York: Garden City Publishers, 1977. Cited in "Can The Mothers Speak?: The Mothers' League of Central High and the 'Bogey' of Inter-Racial Relations" by Phoebe Godfrey, Ph.D., submitted to *Journal of Women's History*, 2003. http://www.newschool.edu/gf/historymatters/papers/ conf03_phoebegodfrey.pdf (Accessed Oct. 6, 2003.)

p. 95, par. 4, John Wyllie, *Post News Talk*: "Conversations in the South," March 3, 1959, 2; CBC, 354 Jarvis St., Toronto, Orval Faubus Collection, series MS F271, 301 box 14, folder 7. Special Collections Division, University of Arkansas Libraries, Fayetteville. Also, FBI interview with Mrs. M. Jackson Sept. 6 and 7, 1957, Sara A. Murphy Papers, series MC 1321, box 9, folder 5, Special Collections Division, University of Arkansas Libraries, Fayetteville. Cited in "Can The Mothers Speak?"

p. 96, par. 3–p. 97, par. 1, Wyllie, *Post News Talk*, 1959; Special Collections Division, University of Arkansas Libraries, Fayetteville. Cited in "Can The Mothers Speak?"

p. 97, par. 1, FBI interview with Mrs. O. R. Aaron Sept. 5, 1957, Sara A. Murphy Papers, series MC 1321, box 9, folder 5, Special Collections Division, University of Arkansas Libraries, Fayetteville. Cited in "Can The Mothers Speak?"

p. 97, par. 2, Arkansas Democrat and Arkansas Gazette, April 13, 1955. http://www.ardemgaz.com/prev/central/CHSmain.html (Accessed Sept. 23, 2003.)

p. 98, par. 5–p. 99, par. 1, Melba Pattillo Beals. *Warriors Don't Cry: A Searing Memoir of the Battle to Integrate Little Rock's Central High*. New York: Washington Square Press, 1995.

p. 99, par. 2, *Indian Express Newspapers*, Aug. 9, 1999. http://www.express india.com/ie/daily/19990809/ile09099.html (Accessed Oct. 1, 2003.)

p. 100, par. 1, "Opening Doors and Minds," *PBS Newshour*, Sept. 25, 1997. http://www.pbs.org/newshour/bb/race_relations/july-dec97/ rock_9-25.html, (Accessed Oct. 1, 2003.)

pp. 101–104, Eileen McCluskey, "Ruby Bridges evokes tears, smiles as she tells her tale." *Harvard Gazette* archives, April 25, 2002.

p. 104, par. 2, *The Toronto Star*, May 25, 2000.

p. 106, par. 4, John F. Kennedy, "Commencement Address at San Diego State College," June 6, 1963. http://www.presidency.ucsb.edu/site/docs/pppus.php?admin=035&year=1963&id=226 (Accessed May 12, 2004.)

p. 107, par. 1, Richard Kluger. *Simple Justice*. New York: Alfred A. Knopf, 1976.

p. 108, par. 2, *Griffin* v. *School Board*, 377 U.S. 218 (1964).

p. 108, par. 3, *Green* v. *County School Board of New Kent County*, 391 U.S. 430 (1968).

Chapter 8

p. 110, par. 2, *Alexander* v. *Board of Education*, 396 U.S. 19 (1969).

p. 111, par. 3–p. 112, par. 1, *Swann* v. *Charlotte-Mecklenburg Board of Education*, 402 U.S. 1 (1971).

p. 113, par. 2, *Wall Street Journal*, July 21, 1999.

p. 113, par. 3, *Ed. Magazine*, Harvard Graduate School of Education, Sept. 1, 2000. http://www.gse.harvard.edu/news/features/busing09012000_page3.html (Accessed Oct. 1, 2003.)

p. 114–p. 115, par. 1, *The New York Times*, Jan. 13, 2002.

p. 115, par. 2, *The New York Times*, March 27, 2002.

p. 115, par. 3–5, *The New York Times*, March 30, 2003.

p. 115, par. 6, Yonkers public schools Web site. http://www.yonkers publicschools.org/Inside_pages/SKLS/22.htm (Accessed May 12, 2004.)

p. 116, par. 4, *Milliken* v. *Bradley*, 418 U.S. 717 (1974).

p. 118, par. 2, *Board of Education of Oklahoma City* v. *Dowell*, 498 U.S. 237 (1991).

p. 118, par. 3, *Freeman* v. *Pitts*, 498 U.S. 1081 (1992).

p. 119, par. 3–p. 120, par. 1, *University of California Regents* v. *Bakke*, 438 U.S. 265 (1978).

p. 120, par. 3–4, *The New York Times*, June 24, 2003.

p. 120, par. 5–p. 121, par. 1, *Grutter* v. *Bollinger* , 539 U.S. __ (2003).

p. 121, par. 3–p. 122, par. 2, Erica Frankenberg, Chungmei Lee, and Gary Orfield. "A Multiracial Society with Segregated Schools: Are We Losing the Dream?" The Civil Rights Project, Harvard University, Jan. 2003. http://www.civilrightsproject.harvard.edu/research/resego3/resegregation03.php (Accessed Oct. 1, 2003.)

p. 122, par. 3, *Wall Street Journal*, July 21, 1999.

p. 122, par. 4, "Opening Doors and Minds," *PBS Newshour*, Sept. 25, 1997. http://www.pbs.org/newshour/bb/race_relations/july-dec97/rock_9-25.html (Accessed Oct. 1, 2003.)

p. 122, par. 5, David Pitts. "*Brown* v. *Board of Education*: The Supreme Court Decision That Changed a Nation," *Issues of Democracy*, vol. 4, no. 2, Sept. 1999. http://usinfo.state.gov/journals/itdhr/0999/ijde/pitts.htm (Accessed Sept. 11, 2003.)

further information

FURTHER READING

Balkin, Jack M. *What* Brown v. Board of Education *Should Have Said: The Nation's Top Legal Experts Rewrite America's Landmark Civil Rights Decision*. New York: New York University Press, 2001.

Bridges, Ruby. *Through My Eyes*. New York: Scholastic, 1999.

Cornelius, Kay. *The Supreme Court* (Your Government: How It Works). Broomall, PA: Chelsea House Pub., 2000.

Fireside, Harvey, and Sarah Betsy Fuller. *Brown v. Board of Education: Equal Schooling for All* (Landmark Supreme Court Cases). Berkeley Heights, NJ: Enslow Publishers, 1994.

Heath, David, and Charlotte Wilcox. *The Supreme Court of the United States* (American Civics). Mankato, MN: Bridgestone Books, 1999.

Levert, Suzanne. *The Supreme Court*. New York: Benchmark Books, 2002.

Patrick, John J. *The Supreme Court of the United States: A Student Companion* (Oxford Student Companions to American Government), second ed. New York: Oxford University Press Children's Books, 2002.

Sanders, Mark C. *Supreme Court* (American Government Today Series). Austin, TX: Raintree/Steck-Vaughn Publishers, 2001.

WEB SITES

Administrative Office of the U.S. Courts
http://www.uscourts.gov/

The African American Registry
http://www.aaregistry.com

American Court Flow Chart System
http://www.judicial.state.ia.us/students/6/

"American Memory," Historical Collections for the National Digital
Library, Library of Congress
http://memory.loc.gov

American Treasures of the Library of Congress
http://lcweb.loc.gov/exhibits/treasures/trr007.html

Brown Foundation for Educational Equity, Excellence and Research,
Washburn University Law Library, Topeka, Kansas
http://brownvboard.org

Brown v. Board Of Education National Historic Site, National Park Service
http://www.nps.gov/brvb/

The Civil Rights Project, Harvard University
http://www.civilrightsproject.harvard.edu/research/resego3/
resegregationo3.php

"Documents Related to Brown v. Board of Education," National
Archives and Records Administration's Digital Classroom
http://www.archives.gov/digital_classroom/lessons/brown_v_board_
documents/brown_v_board.html

FindLaw
http://www.findlaw.com

"The History of Jim Crow"
http://www.jimcrowhistory.org

"Landmark Cases: Supreme Court," Street Law and the Supreme Court Historical Society
http://www.landmarkcases.org/brown/courtsystem.html

"Opening Doors and Minds," PBS Newshour, Sept. 25, 1997.
http://www.pbs.org/newshour/bb/race_relations/july-dec97/rock_9-25.html

The Oyez Project: U.S. Supreme Court Multimedia
http://www.oyez.org/oyez/frontpage

"The Rise and Fall of Jim Crow," PBS
http://www.pbs.org/wnet/jimcrow/

Supreme Court Historical Society
http://www.supremecourthistory.org

BIBLIOGraPHY

BOOKS AND ARTICLES

The Association of Teachers' Web sites. "Education and Civil Rights in America 1945 to 1968." http://www.historylearningsite.co.uk/USAeduc.htm (Accessed Sept. 11, 2003.)

Beals, Melba Pattillo. *Warriors Don't Cry: A Searing Memoir of the Battle to Integrate Little Rock's Central High*. New York: Washington Square Press, 1995.

"Busing in Boston: Looking Back at the History and Legacy," *Ed. Magazine*, Harvard Graduate School of Education, Sept. 1, 2000.

Citron, Rodger D. "The Case of the Century: A Review of a New Book on Caste, Culture, and *Brown* v. *Board of Education*." *FindLaw's Writ Book Reviews*, Dec. 5, 2003. http://writ.news.findlaw.com/books/reviews/20031205_citron.html

Clark, Associate Justice Tom C. "Memorandum to Supreme Court Justices." Tom C. Clark Papers, U.S. Supreme Court Case Files. Box A2, Folder 3. Rare Books & Special Collections, Tarlton Law Library, University of Texas at Austin. http://www.law.du.edu/russell/lh/sweatt/docs/clarkmemo.htm (Accessed Sept. 16, 2003.)

Coles, Robert. *The Ruby Bridges Story*. New York: Scholastic, 1995.

Cottrol, Robert J., Raymond T. Diamond, and Leland B. Ware. Brown v. Board of Education: *Caste, Culture, and the Constitution*. Kansas: University Press of Kansas, 2003.

Defender (Chicago), May 18, 1954.
http://www.landmarkcases.org/brown/reaction.html
(Accessed Sept. 11, 2003.)

Elliot, Louise. *Toronto Star*, May 25, 2000.

Fairclough, Adam. *Better Day Coming: Blacks and Equality, 1890–2000*.
New York: Viking Press, 2001.

Fassett, John B. "Mr. Justice Reed and *Brown* v. *Board of Education*,"
Supreme Court Historical Society 1986 Yearbook. http://www.supreme-
courthistory.org/04_library/subs_volumes /04_c18_k.html
(Accessed May. 11, 2004.)

Frankenberg, Erica, Chungmei Lee, and Gary Orfield. "A Multiracial
Society with Segregated Schools: Are We Losing the Dream?" The
Civil Rights Project, Harvard University, Jan. 2003.

Fribourg, Marjorie G. *The Supreme Court in American History: Ten Great
Decisions—The People, the Times and the Issues*. Philadelphia: Macrae
Smith Company, 1965.

"The Gallup Poll: 65 Years of Polling History—Timeline Of Polling
History: Events That Shaped the United States, and the World,"
Gallup Organization.
http://www.gallup.com/content?c:=9967 (Accessed June 1, 2004.)

Godfrey, Phoebe, Ph.D., "Can The Mothers Speak?: The Mothers'
League of Central High and the 'Bogey' of Inter-Racial Relations.
Submitted to *Journal of Women's History*, 2003.
http://www.newschool.edu/gf/historymatters/papers/conf03_
phoebegodfrey.pdf (Accessed Oct. 6, 2003.)

Hall, Ruby Bridges. "The Education of Ruby Nell." *Guideposts*, March 2000.

Herda, D. J. *Mr. Chief Justice: Earl Warren and the Reticence of America*
http://amsaw.org/swetkyagency/submissionsynopsis-herda-justice-
series-earlwarren.html
(Accessed May 12, 2004.)

Hunter-Gault, Charlayne, with Ruby Bridges Hall. "A Class of One."
Online *NewsHour*, PBS, Feb. 18, 1997.

Irons, Peter. *Jim Crow's Children: The Broken Promise of the* Brown
Decision. New York: Viking, 2002.

Jacoby, Tamar. "Beyond Busing," *Wall Street Journal*, July 21, 1999.

Kluger, Richard. *Simple Justice*. New York: Alfred A. Knopf, 1976.

Kurland, Philip B., and Gerhard Casper. *Landmark Briefs and Arguments of the Supreme Court of the United States: Constitutional Law*, "Brown *v*. Board of Education (1954 & 1955)," vol. 49 & 49A. Arlington, VA: University Publications of America Inc., 1975.

Linder, Douglas O. "Before *Brown*: Charles H. Houston and the Gaines Case," Famous Trials. University of Missouri-Kansas City School of Law, 2000.
http://www.law.umkc.edu/faculty/projects/ftrials/conlaw/houstonessay.html
(Accessed Jan. 10, 2003.)

McCluskey, Eileen. "Ruby Bridges evokes tears, smiles as she tells her tale." *Harvard Gazette* archives.

"The Murder of Emmett Till," *American Experience*, PBS Online.
http://www.pbs.org
(Accessed Sept. 12, 2003.)

The New York Times, Dec. 13, 1938, May 18, 1954, Jan. 13, 2002, March 27, 2002, March 30, 2003, June 24, 2003.

"Opening Doors and Minds," *PBS Newshour*, Sept. 25, 1997.
http://www.landmarkcases.org/brown/reaction.html
(Accessed Sept. 11, 2003.)

Patterson, James T. Brown *v*. Board of Education: *A Civil Rights Milestone and Its Troubled Legacy*. London: Oxford University Press, 2001.

Pettys, Dick. "Former Georgia Governor Herman Talmadge dies at 88," Associated Press, March 21, 2002.

Pitts, David. "Brown *v*. Board of Education: *The Supreme Court Decision That Changed A Nation*," Issues of Democracy, vol. 4, no. 2, Sept. 1999.

Roberts, Paul Craig, and Lawrence M. Stratton. *The Brown Decision, The New Color Line: How Quotas and Privileges Destroy Democracy*. Washington, DC: Regnery Publishing, 1997.
http://www.lewrockwell.com/orig/brown.html
(Accessed June 1, 2003.)

Schwartz, Bernard. *Swann's Way: The School Busing Case and the Supreme Court.* New York: Oxford University Press, 1986.

Totenberg, Nina. "The Supreme Court and *Brown* v. *Board of Ed.*: The Deliberations Behind the Landmark 1954 Ruling," National Public Radio. http://www.npr.org/display_pages/features/feature_1537409.html (Accessed May 11, 2004.)

The United States Law Week, Vol. 18, No. 39, p. 3277, April 11, 1950.

University of Missouri-Columbia. "A History of the University of Missouri." http://www.missouri.edu/~vawww.history/ (Accessed June 1, 2004.)

Weinberg, Meyer. *A Chance to Learn: The History of Race and Education in the United States.* New York: Cambridge University Press, 1977.

Wicker, Tom. *Dwight D. Eisenhower.* New York: Times Books/Henry Holt & Company, 2002.

Williams, Juan. "Marshall's Law," *Washington Post Magazine,* Jan. 7, 1990. http://www.thurgoodmarshall.com/speeches/tmlaw_article.htm (Accessed May 12, 2004.)

Wilson, Paul. *A Time to Lose: Representing Kansas.* Lawrence, Kansas: University of Kansas Press, 1995.

List of cases and statutes related to *Brown* v. *Board of Education*

Alexander v. *Holmes County Board of Education*, 396 U.S. 19 (1969)

Belton v. *Gebhart*, 87 A. 2d 862 (Del. Ch. 1952)

Berea College v. *Kentucky*, 211 U.S. 45 (1908)

Board of Education of Oklahoma City v. *Dowell*, 498 U.S. 237 (1991)

Bolling v. *Sharpe*, 347 U.S. 497 (1954)

Briggs v. *Elliott*, 347 U.S. 497 (1954)

Brown v. *Board of Education of Topeka*, 347 U.S. 483 (1954)

Brown v. *Board of Education of Topeka*, 349 U.S. 294 (1955)

Bulah v. *Gebhart*, 87 A. 2d 862 (Del. Ch. 1952)

Commonwealth of Kentucky v. *Berea College*, No. 6009 (Madison Cty. Cir. Ct. Feb. 7, 1905)

Dorothy E. Davis v. *County School Board of Prince Edward County*, 347 U.S. 483 (1954)

Fifth, Thirteenth, Fourteenth, Fifteenth, Twenty-Fourth Amendments, U.S. Constitution

Freeman v. *Pitts*, 498 U.S. 1081 (1992)

Gayle v. *Browder*, 352 U.S. 903 (1956)

Gebhart v. *Belton*, 91 A.2d 137 (1952)

Gebhart v. *Bulah*, 87 A.2d 862 (1952)

Gratz v. *Bollinger*, No. 02-516.

Green v. *County School Board of New Kent County, Va.*, 391 U.S. 430 (1968)

Griffin v. *School Board*, 377 U.S. 218 (1964)

McLaurin v. *Oklahoma State Regents for Higher Education*, 339 U.S. 637 (1950)

Meyer v. *Nebraska*, 262 U.S. 390 (1923)

Milliken v. *Bradley*, 418 U.S. 717 (1974)

Missouri Ex Rel. Gaines v. *Canada, Registrar of the University of Missouri, et al.*, 305 U.S. 337 (1938)

Plessy v. *Ferguson*, 163 US 537 (1896)

Roberts v. *City of Boston*, 59 Mass. 198, 5 Cush. 198 (1849)

Sipuel v. *Board of Regents*, 332 U.S. 631 (1948)

Southern Manifesto, 1956

Swann v. *Charlotte-Mecklenburg Board of Education*, 402 U.S. 1 (1971)

Sweatt v. *Painter*, 339 U.S. 629 (1950)

U.S. v. *Reese*, 92 U.S. 214 (1876)

index

Page numbers in **boldface** are illustrations, tables, and charts

about the author

susan DUDLeY GOLD has written more than three dozen books for middle-school and high-school students on a variety of topics, including American history, health issues, law, and space. Her most recent works for Benchmark Books are *Gun Control* in the Open for Debate series, and *Roe v. Wade: A Woman's Choice?*, *Brown v. Board of Education: Separate but Equal?*, and *The Pentagon Papers: National Security or the Right to Know*—all in the Supreme Court Milestones series. She is currently working on three more books about Supreme Court cases.

Susan Gold has also written several books on Maine history. Among her many careers in journalism are stints as a reporter for a daily newspaper, managing editor of two statewide business magazines, and free-lance writer for several regional publications. She and her husband, John Gold, own and operate a Web design and publishing business. Susan has received numerous awards for her writing and design work. In 2001 she received a Jefferson Award for community service in recognition of her work with a support group for people with chronic pain, which she founded in 1993. Susan and her husband, also a children's book author, live in Maine. They have one son, Samuel.